This project is dedicated to every woman that decided not to give up on her dreams!

Table of Contents

Introduction

When you bring together a group of like-minded individuals, the limit of what is possible begins to fade away and the possibilities grow! When I decided to do this book collaboration project it was not because it has not been done before, but I wanted the work put into a project like this to have meaning, to own a strong sense of purpose. When the moment of clarity came to me for my own next steps in business and the work I was curating, I began to see the bigger picture and received a prompting that NOW is the time to begin a journey with a chosen group. Many women want to share their story in a greater way but don't know how to begin. I knew that everyone chosen for this project would have the potential to go on to do a solo project and I wanted to equip them with the tools I know they did not already have in order to get them on their way.

In the USA, it seems that there is no shortage of women empowerment groups. But the distinction (which will not only be seen and heard but felt) comes from the motivation behind the why! *A Purpose Driven Woman* is distinct to women that are choosing to be successful and unapologetic in their careers, businesses, and lives. The women in this project share a message of motivation, of truth and authenticity.

Too often we've tried to separate our career and business from our home lives. I've learned that we take ourselves—our mindset, our points of view, our hopes, our dreams, our skills, our talents—everywhere that we go. We will share in this book how we've been able to accomplish a self-defined level of success. You're going to be moved, inspired to live with intention and purpose, and provoked to walk out your truth.

The Path to Purpose

Felicia Shakespeare

I must say these last three years have been a complete whirlwind for me. Stretching myself, doing things I've never done before, and experiencing life in a much richer way has been a very high priority. As I think through the series of events that have taken place over these last three years, I've asked myself: *At what point did things in my life begin to shift? When did it all begin to change?* I was able to trace everything in this timeframe back to one thing—a decision. When you think about the complexity of today's society, our world is primarily based on the courage someone had to make something new, think something new, or become something new. The decision that I made to move beyond my own limitations of self-doubt, self-sabotage, and insecurity have all propelled me to charter a path to purpose that I never fully understood until I got on it. And I don't mean purpose in the traditional sense based on a definition I read or heard somewhere. The realization came to me that real purpose is NOT what's in any dictionary; real purpose is identified when one becomes internally free! When I started to internalize the message and the understanding that I owned the solutions all along for what I had been searching for outside of myself, words cannot fully describe this type of liberty! Many of us are searching vigorously for solutions that we fail to realize we already possess. This has been the very reason why I (we) don't do things like everyone else; why I (we) don't interpret or process information as other individuals would. We all bring a unique perspective to the world because of the mere fact that we were distinctly created. No individual holds the exact same set of ideas as the next. Our ideas are unique, down to our very DNA, when compared to billions upon billions of people in the world. The day that I came to this conclusive realization, my energy and the way that I move (which I sometimes refer to as synergy) became different. At that point, I began to naturally gravitate toward things that made me the most fulfilled and gave me peace, and those things began to gravitate to me as well. I decided that enough was enough and I began to move about my life with a sense of urgency because we only receive this one opportunity to exist on Earth. I sincerely believe that God has brought each and every one of us into this world and when motion, movement, and meaning collide we then start to see our purpose. By making one decision, I was propelled onto a trajectory of life that I did not know was possible. Every subsequent decision has allowed me to continue on **the path to purpose**. What I mean by the statement "the path to purpose" is that once your mindset has changed about your situation and the decision is made to be who you were intended to be, somehow the entire direction of your life organically becomes altered and starts leaning in that direction. This can also be true when the opposite behavior begins to occur; things may go in a direction just as easily for the worse. How you see your life will always be the first component to impact your viewpoint or point of view. Outcomes are experienced in your mind well before they manifest around you. I am a firm believer that before you will ever see it, you must "see it."

THE POWER OF INTENTIONALITY

Being intentional is one of the main paths to personal fulfillment. I am a firm believer that in order to make strides toward our dreams or goals, it is very necessary to do so with intention. Intention is an aim or plan of action. One Scripture that has always stood out to me is, "Without a vision, the people perish."—Proverbs 29:18. In my mind, that includes two perspectives—how one actually visualizes something and being a visionary (someone who leads a cause of action). Both of these points of action require two different approaches or skill sets. Having a vision means: I have imagined. Imagination vividly shows the mind what could be. Ultimately, that leads to having hopes and dreams manifested. We have to see it before we actually "see it" as I said before. The latter perspective deals with the process one goes through without having a full understanding of how to accomplish the outcome of what is seen; however, at a minimum, one can get the ball rolling. When I think of both parts of the process, I think of the ladies that I chose for this collaborative project. They are visionaries in their respective spheres of influence. Many people, specifically women, often want to know the "how." Two very prominent business figures who started with nothing and created something are Bill Gates, founder of Microsoft, and Mark Zuckerberg, founder of Facebook. History tells us how each of these men navigated into what ultimately was a part of their purpose, which was changing the face of the technological ecosystem. Prominent female business icon Oprah Winfrey has remained at the top of her game. She started from no to minimal notoriety and became a talk show queen, host, philanthropist, producer, then network owner. Her rise shows the power of being intentional and clear about your purpose. I can only imagine that in the dream stage, each of these individuals had a sense of how great their ideas could be. But you better believe they had no idea that things would go in the direction they did. I believe that each and every one of us is placed here on God's green earth with a unique set of talents, in the way that we think, and what we are sent here to achieve.

The visionary women I chose for this project are beyond ready to share their life-changing messages of when they also made their shift into their purpose. The depth of their experiences will warm your heart, make you think, and set your soul on fire. This book is a testament that if we make the necessary steps to move in our purpose, the light only begins to shine brighter and brighter on our journey. It's clear by all accounts that not only can you reach your goals, but you can also achieve your dreams to become *A Purpose Driven Woman*.

A Kaleidoscope of Contradictory Days that Are Simply Unforgettable

Bella Caetano

Have you ever imagined being born 5,000 miles away from your destiny? That is exactly what happened to me. Let's begin this journey in a small Brazilian town in 1990, a year that we could not anticipate how connected the world would be only three decades later. Imagine a pregnant 15-year-old about to give birth; that was my mom. Not so unusual in a town with less than ten thousand families in the middle of farmlands and woods. My dad was 10 years older than my mom, and he could give her a life. I was given my dad's mom's name. She had passed away a few years earlier. I was named Bella after her. I only know stories about her. I know she was an entrepreneur herself, selling some produce and making natural herbs medicine to cure the poor people in need. Her full name was Bella Ombelina Caetano.

I grew up feeling very lucky to be the first baby in the family to get her name. It was quite nice to be called Bella all the time, which means beautiful in Portuguese just like in Italian. Well, I didn't feel quite as lucky when my parents got divorced. I was 10 years old, I had two younger siblings, and I had a house to take care of. I was cooking and cleaning while my mom worked three jobs to afford the two rooms we were living in. I had to mature very early in life and as expected, I followed the path that was familiar. At age 17, just like my mom, I also got married. I had a huge house, so many rooms, a pool, money to do my nails, and even money to open my first business—a clothing shop. Yes, I had a store when I was only 18. I was able to take my mom and brothers on vacations; I did things I had never dreamed of doing. I had made decent choices, but I was extremely unhappy because that was not actually my dream life. That was what I had to do because I did not know any better, and it kind of worked. There were days filled with colors and also darkness inside of my heart. Luckily, I had no kids. And in the midst of the four years I was married, I started wondering what the world outside of what I knew looked like. I started asking myself questions like: *What if I could travel to other places? What if the answers are not here where I live? What if I could be just as brave as when I decided to get married to try, at least try, to have a better future?* So, that is exactly what I did. I got divorced, sold my store, made a plan, booked a flight, and came to America to start the most interesting chapters of my life.

"Bella, why the United States?" you might ask. Well, there are not many movies about France, Australia, or Germany that are showcased in the afternoons on Brazilian television. In Brazil, we grow up dreaming about a white Christmas; we even have fake snow all over the place. I am not kidding. I grew up watching American movies and dreaming about the American houses with bathtubs (which is not something common in Brazil for a middle-class family) and singing American songs as if I really knew the lyrics (even though I had not learned a word of English yet). These were just a few small things that started my curiosity for the American dream. The more I kept going and exploring, the more I was curious to see and learn. Taking yourself out of your comfort zone makes you wonder more about what is beyond people's personalities and actions. You will never be the same after a culture shock. You learn to appreciate different perspectives. Always give yourself a chance to experiment. I know it can be scary, but you will become a product of your surroundings. It was quite scary to come to the United States without even speaking English, but I was willing to do it because I knew I was going to have my own bathtub in my room and finally touch real snow. I also knew that I would never struggle to sing my favorite songs anymore. I also knew that if I could learn English, I could have better chances of getting a good job when I went back to Brazil; I could even teach English or at least become a better person in general.

I was determined to explore and challenge myself. I had a plan. The plan was to live in the US for six months, learn English, and go back to Brazil to attend architecture school (which was my dream in the first place, but I technically exchanged it for a comfortable and secure marriage). I had great grades. I was always the class leader. I was the girl with the ideas; the fearless one. But I had no clue how I could attend college since no one in my entire family had done it before. The only thing I knew was that getting a good husband was safe and would give me a life. I was actually smart enough to keep myself out of trouble and my mom was very good at putting me in time-out whenever I did something even close to wrong. Because of her, I learned very early on about deadlines, responsibilities, and consequences.

Following the plan, I arrived in Denver, Colorado, in March of 2012, to live for six months with a host family. I made my ex-husband pay the expenses as part of our divorce agreement. I was going to live with them and attend English school five days a week, seven hours a day. After three months of living there, I met my current husband. Of course, back in 2012, I had no idea I was going to marry him. I could barely speak English and I was definitely not letting another man change the course of my life. My days in Colorado were magical. There were so many new things I was getting to learn. I was completely in love with my host family. I actually got a chance to be a daughter again without many responsibilities. I got to just experience life without having to worry about picking up my brothers from school on time or having to consider what my entire little town would think of a married woman doing silly things. I was free and very far from where people would gossip about my life. I got to be myself. I did fall in love with Tommy, my current husband, but remember the plan? Yeah, the day to go home arrived and I did not even feel guilty about breaking up with him. All I could think was that I had lived so much in such a small period of time. I was full of ideas and I had the energy to rebuild my life.

I went back to Brazil and attended an architecture school in São Paulo for four years. So much happened in those years. I had fun, I danced a lot, I modeled as a side gig, I made a ton of friends for life, I got back with Tommy and broke up with him many times, I went through having an eating disorder, I had a serious breakdown and ended up in a hospital diagnosed with schizophrenia, I had countless frustrating dates, I got very disappointed with what architecture really is, and many days and nights I debated with myself about what I was doing with my life. During those years, I was far from my family because they were living in Mato Grosso, my home state, and I was also living far from Tommy whom I could never take completely out of my thoughts. It was again colorful memories with lots of dark ones. I started wondering: *Is my life always going to be like this? Am I always going to live these happy days until I sabotage myself one more time?* I was so hopeless that I started wondering: *What if I had just stayed married, kept my shop, stayed close to my family, and never lived out my dreams?* Well, now it was too late for that; it was not an option anymore. The reality was that I had this unstable long-distance relationship with Tommy, I was still attending architecture school (and not really liking it), and to be very honest, I was debating where life would really take me. Tommy could not afford to get married and take care of us and I had no money, half of a degree, and not enough courage to figure out how to move to another country. I was lost and hopeless. All I had was my faith in God. So, just like every other time in my life when I had no strength, I would just put my life in His hands and pray. But I had days that I would forget that God existed. I had days when it was easier to just not believe anymore. I had days when not following God's rules was more convenient. And I had days when I had no choice but to kneel down, cry a lot, say I'm sorry, and pray.

It was New Year's Day. Tommy and I had gotten back together and he was visiting me in Brazil. He got a call from the Chicago Fire Department telling him he was selected out of 17,000 applicants to be among the very first 100 people to start the job. Was it my miracle? Was it what I was waiting for? We did not know yet, but it at least gave us hope. Tommy had to buy a last-minute ticket for a return flight because he had to be back in the US in three days to get the position. He went back, got the job, and the following year we were getting married. I quit architecture school, moved to Chicago, and of course I had a plan again. Would it actually work this time? Well, I had no clue, but I knew I had to have one. I thought about what I could do with the set of skills life had given me on all of those very contradictory days. So many unfinished goals, so many random things I got to learn, so many disconnected pieces of information and people I got to meet. I had very long days and nights of procrastination and thinking until I got to a conclusion, or at least a piece of it to start.

I really did not know that God was placing me where I had to be to learn what I had to learn. From almost four years of architecture school, I had a good knowledge of design. I knew I was smart enough to figure out production, logistics, and the import system. Since this would not be my first time venturing out on the business route, I had an old contact from when I had a shop, a great jewelry manufacturer in the south of Brazil. It was hard to believe that this old contact from a turbulent chapter of my life could change my life.

I could not work while Tommy and I were dealing with the immigration process, so that gave me time to come up with a name for my company. I ended up using my grandma's middle and last name since I already had the first one in my own documents. I knew this project would be for life, so I made sure to register the name, create a logo, and start building my brand identity.

When I first moved to Chicago in 2016, I brought with me some very simple jewelry designs that I figured out how to produce by assembling pre-made materials. I dreamed about my collection with natural stones, but all I could afford were some beads and cubic zirconias. My designs were not nearly as good as the ones I had planned to have, but the manufacturer I wanted to work with in Brazil needed a large quantity to open an order for me and I had no money or customers. Plus, I was moving to a new city I had no idea how to navigate. When I got to Chicago, I spent tons of hours taking pictures of my simple jewelry and posting them, along with my name and logo, on Brazilian Facebook groups. I attended every Brazilian networking event I could find in town. I was lucky enough to come across MOSTRA the Brazilian Film Festival and started volunteering as many hours as I had available. Shortly after, I was invited to become a board member of Partners of the Americas and my network was being built among the Brazilian community, enough to start hosting some small jewelry parties. I worked at a shoe store part-time to meet new customers and

I convinced the owner to let me bring in my jewelry and sell it along with the shoes. I babysat to get some extra money to attend markets and trunk shows. I did everything I could to put my name out there. Finally, in January of 2018, I incorporated as an LLC by myself (after many nights researching how to do it in a country where the only documents I had were a green card and a work permit). Could I become a business owner and an importer or even compete and succeed here? All those questions were being answered one by one, and I was building my company step by step. Once I incorporated my business, many things changed. I was able to get a 30-day popup shop on Michigan Avenue. In those 30 days, I made enough money to pay for two more months and stay in the shop to launch my very first collection. All designed by me with natural stones from Brazil, from the manufacturer of my dreams, with the quality of my dreams. My popup shop was quite a success and I was able to stay there. It was my first permanent location and the first Brazilian boutique in Chicago.

I realized that I talked about Brazil so much that I fell in love with it. When I first had the idea of opening my business in 2016, I thought I was going to design jewelry. Now, my main mission is to create jobs in Brazil, and sharing Brazilian culture with customers has become my passion. People know so little about my country and there is so much there to be explored. I want to change that. And after all I have been through, I have no doubt that it is just a matter of time before the world knows about Brazilian design, art, and culture.

As my final words, I have to say that in many ways life does not make any sense. But if you are fearless and let yourself be bold, you will for certain learn the set of skills you need to accomplish what you were called to do. When I look back over my life, all I see is a kaleidoscope of memories that I will never forget. So, don't be afraid of yourself, be gracefully bold.

Daydream in Color and Pursue Greatness

~

Charisma Smith

LIVING YOUR DREAM

Although I knew I would one day become an awesome business owner, I could not discount my journey with corporate America. It was my corporate training and experiences that led to my love and passion for real estate.

The turning point in my journey was initiated on one unforgettable day in church. During that service, my pastor said, "Pursue all that God has for you!!!! Stop being scared." At that point, I realized I had to activate my faith, and those words served as the encouragement needed to push me towards my destiny. Now don't get me wrong, I didn't just jump out there. I was practicing real estate in the evenings and weekends before I gave my final notice to my corporate job. The Word of God advises in Luke 14:28 that it is foolishness to start a project without first estimating the cost and coming up with a working plan. I knew God bestowed upon me gifts and desires that exceeded the limitations found in a corporate setting. I finally accepted that entrepreneurship is not God's secondary plan, it is my ultimate plan. No more second guesses or struggles; entrepreneurship is the will of God for the dreamer. The truth was that I was stuck in a box called corporate America, which rendered me powerless in my plight. My daydreams of entrepreneurship were calling... and although challenged, I answered. My passion forced me to launch out without a clear plan and direction.

That sermon motivated me to start a real estate company with my college friend and sorority sister. After 17 years, she continues to be the smartest business partner that one could ever desire. We both worked for the same banking institution 17 years ago. I remember the day that I called her to inform her that it was time to pursue what God had placed us on this earth to do. That decision was my very first step into entrepreneurship and actualizing my dream of being a business owner.

I had a plan mapped out. I saved about six months of my salary. We also went to the bank and got a line of credit for the business. We scoped out an office space and opened our office. Although the future wasn't so bright at the beginning, there was an assurance that I was on the path to destiny. I can recall all of the emotions I felt during that time of pursuit. It was a combination of zeal, fear, and enthusiasm. I don't advise anyone with these same dreams to leave your job without a clear roadmap or plan. No glorious feat is ever accomplished by coincidence; there is always time for proper preparation.

Entrepreneurs need broad critical thinking skills to ensure a successful company. Most wear various roles at the core of their business. Owners would describe themselves as multifaceted. A successful business person should consider the different factors of running a business from accounting, human resources, marketing, securing capital funding, and business and strategic planning to scale your business. Know the areas where you have limited strengths because, ultimately, you are responsible for a quality operation. You must practice different habits to be effective along your journey. The first step of the dream chaser is to believe in yourself and your dreams and allow your mind to manifest good thoughts. Then, determine your purpose and always believe that you are special. You have something unique to offer the world. The most challenging part of dream chasing is putting in the work. In my corporate job, I worked between the hours of 8:00 a.m.-5:00 p.m. As an entrepreneur doing real estate, I worked until the job was done. I remember burning the candle at both ends and getting very little sleep. I would take a nap at 10:00 p.m. and get back up at 2:00 a.m. or 3:00 a.m. to complete my work before my daily routine started. I was tired, but the adrenaline kept me going. I could not faint or get weary; this was my destiny.

My biggest fears were not being financially stable and not being ready to transition from corporate America to entrepreneurship. I was still responsible for maintaining my mortgage, car payment, and other personal expenses. My initial goal was to become a leading minority-owned boutique real estate firm providing clients with exceptional customer service. Included in my business plan were goals to create a multifaceted company that expanded into various areas of real estate. I had to help keep the roof over my head, make car payments, and keep food on the table. This plan had to be right, and it had to work. My business partner and I, both former corporate project managers, had regularly scheduled meetings to create the plan and a strategy for how to manifest it. I would ask myself, *How many deals do I have to put together to equal my current salary so that I don't cause hardship in my home?* Money was a critical factor in my decision.

The next challenge was defining my purpose. Why did I want to create this business? What joy would it bring? What would make me wake up every morning and work, even if I didn't receive money for two to three months? What kind of impact could I make on the world? What would be my legacy? I would be remiss if I did not discuss the role of fear. Finding answers to all of those questions as part of the journey liberated me and renewed my strength. I embraced my new life with confidence and enthusiasm. I was unstoppable! Failure was not an option.

DREAMS DELAYED

Entrepreneurship is the fire that brightens my day and lights up my spirit. It is like a flame that consumes me day in and day out. It's not always an easy road adorned with rose petals and flowers, but it is a perfect path to glory. For instance, one of the darkest moments of my life was when I found my father deceased on the floor only weeks after burying my stepmother, his wife of over 35 years. Just a few years later, I became a widow.

That was the true turning point in my life. Prior to that, I was moving along as a successful entrepreneur for some years and our company was growing steadily. We achieved our initial goal of incorporating a real estate firm, and we continued to expand our team. As a result, we were able to pursue other business opportunities. We learned a lot during those business transitions. They laid the foundation for future partnerships. The death of your loved ones can knock the air right out of your lungs, and multiple deaths can bring you to your knees. It can make you question your relationship with God and your existence. I often wondered whether I should continue this path of entrepreneurship because I was overwhelmed and drained. But, once you decide to fight for purpose, your whole outlook changes.

Through God's grace, prayer, friends and family, and a loyal business partner, I regained my footing. I rededicated my life to living on purpose. I could still see my dream through my circumstances. I knew that as an entrepreneur, I would have a positive impact on the world. I had to reach people to help them achieve the American dream of homeownership, create legacy wealth, and generate jobs to hire people in the community. I was convinced that my destiny was more significant than my present situation. I developed a resilient mindset; it propelled me in the right direction. What was meant to steal my dream gave me zeal. I realized that the only time you have on this earth is what you're given. Live life to the fullest.

Today, I am co-owner of a thriving boutique real estate firm. As time progressed, we expanded our business to include a construction company because it paired so well with real estate. Our latest venture is a non-profit focused on affordable housing. As I reflect on my journey, I will admit that it has been challenging. I am certainly no stranger to pain, failure, and disappointment. Yet, as spoken so eloquently by Eleanor Roosevelt, "The future belongs to those who believe in the beauty of their dreams."

Through the highs and lows, I have maintained my focus by holding firm to my dreams, passion, and purpose. While my experiences have been eventful and often tragic, I remain a product of grace and a testimony of God's blessings and favor.

PURSUING GREATNESS

People often ask me questions like: "What are your tips for becoming a successful entrepreneur?" "How do I start a business?" "What must I do to move my business or career to the next level?" My reply to such questions is always very straightforward: "You need to know that it takes faith, prayer, meditation (quiet time), discipline, and most importantly, actions (steps) to accomplish your goals. You have to also discover your passion and the potential profit it can yield in the marketplace. Carving out a niche for yourself in a densely competitive market will also give you an edge over others.

Research and deliberate planning are indispensable prerequisites for any progressive business. One of the enduring lessons I learned in life is never to take anything for granted. The pieces of information that comes your way, your experiences, successes, failures, or ah-ha moments should be treasured. Your attitude determines your altitude in life. Entrepreneurship can be draining at times, but optimism will ease you of great burdens as you go. As an entrepreneur, there are times my day does not go as planned, but it's ok; I try to be very careful and watch the words that come out of my mouth and the attitude that I project. Your attitude and your language can change your situation.

Lastly, surround yourself with positive people and mentors, attend seminars, and gather great reading materials. Associate with like-minded people who can positively speak into your life. Find mentors that can guide your steps so that you don't make unnecessary mistakes; those mentors will also help to open doors for you. Going to conferences and seminars and gathering great reading materials will stretch you, grow you, and open your mind to a different level of thinking. Someone in the universe is waiting for you to start your business idea and move in the direction of your destiny. What are you waiting for?

Sometimes people ask me if I have "Black Girl Magic" pertaining to entrepreneurship. To be honest, I follow simple principles in life. Here's what I do:

- I write out the vision or the goal
- I map out the steps it will take to accomplish my vision or goal
- I speak action items into fruition (Your language can change your situation.)
- I pursue the vision
- I maintain positive thoughts and good energy (Positivity goes a long way toward influencing your destiny.)
- I believe only good things are coming to me
- I stay optimistic (Optimism is a formidable weapon on the route to greatness.)
- I visualize myself already "there"
- I do not allow negative thinking to take over my mind
- I see myself in abundance

- I keep the right attitude (Remember, attitude determines your altitude in life.)
- I practice gratitude (Practice gratitude regularly—daily or weekly.)

You should keep a written or online journal of things you are thankful for throughout your day or when your day is over. Write your experiences down or say them out loud. For example: "I'm grateful that I met a new person that could be a mentor." "I'm grateful I submitted my documents to the Secretary of State for my incorporation paperwork." "I'm grateful that I met a great banker who explained and approved my line of credit for my new business," etc. Thankfulness gives you more energy and being grateful fills your spirit with greater joy and motivation.

One of my favorite Scriptures in the Bible is Jeremiah 29:11: "For I know the plans I have for you," says the LORD. "They are plans for good and not for disaster, to give you a future and a hope." That Scripture alone gives me confidence even when I'm in low moments of life. I have to look towards the future with hope.

Be fearless, be strong, and be courageous on the journey of entrepreneurship. Fear is a dangerous disease that stagnates a giant on the spot and keeps a man within the confines of mediocrity.

Expect endless possibilities and opportunities every day. Open your mouth and speak life, focus your mind on that goal, and believe that the vision you have in front of you will be accomplished. If you can conceive a vision, you can achieve it, if only you believe. These are working principles in my life, and if you carefully apply them to your life, you are on your way to fulfilling your dreams and finding your purpose.

How the Game of Golf Helped Me Reinvent Myself

Erika "Birdie" Shavers

It was a quiet evening sitting in my home office. Tears welled up in my eyes and I was extremely frightened because I was not sure if I wanted to proceed with what I was thinking.

But I needed help. I needed to release my shame and guilt and turn it over to God.

I prayed and meditated over the decision and cannot recall at this writing if I asked anyone's opinion or not. But it was time to make a decision... it was now or never.

SEND!

I did it! I hit the send button to over 30-40 people asking for help with my situation. I was nervous and relieved at the same time. I remember going to sleep that night feeling proud that I had the courage to ask for help. I finally came to the realization that I have the resources of friends and sorority sisters that if able they would help me. That is what family, friendship, and sisterhood is all about.

It was the voice of the Lord that told me, "I can do all things through Christ which strengthens me."—Philippians 4:13

Every single morning when I woke up, I recited that Scripture. I truly believe that it gave me the strength to move on and persevere. This is my story.

I am a huge fan of self-help books. I've read everything from *The Game of Life* by Florence Scovel Shinn, *How Successful People Think* by John C. Maxwell, *The Power of Positive Thinking* by Norman Vincent Peale, to *Think and Grow Rich* by Napoleon Hill, and the list goes on and on. When I was in the real estate profession, I was *in* real estate. Acquiring property, rehabbing, and becoming a landlord was what I was passionate about. I enjoyed it to the fullest. It was a successful journey, but not without struggles, setbacks, and emotional tension among business partners. You could not tell me I wasn't living the life in my little bubble.

That all came crashing down before my eyes in 2007. Yep! It sure did. Looking back, I have to admit I overextended myself. Being in the game of real estate and mortgages, I knew the ins and outs of acquiring and financing real estate. *WTH* was I thinking?! That's just it... I went from thinking to just doing. And I paid a hefty price. One I have no intention of reliving. I had become successful at manifesting my dreams. Anything I set my mind to do, I did it! I had close to a million dollars in assets, credit cards, real estate, etc., and a decent savings. And then I lost everything. How did I not see this coming? Or perhaps, I just ignored the signs and thought I would figure it out somehow.

Perhaps you are thinking, *How does this experience with real estate have anything to do with golf?* Well, it's not the real estate experience that has anything to do with golf, but more about how I survived (in my mind) the embarrassing and unfortunate situation of having to move back in with family at the age of 44 years old, after building a successful career in real estate, and humbling myself to ask for financial assistance. That experience actually catapulted me into developing the courage to not only ask for help, but to believe that if I needed anything in life all I had to do was ask.

During that time, I was downsized from my position in the mortgage industry and I felt alone and disgusted. Perhaps I took on too much trying to realize my dream. My overall goal in life was not to end up living paycheck to paycheck. My brothers and I weren't completely poor growing up, but we weren't rich or middle class either. I vowed to do more than just survive. I had become an entrepreneur and I was proud of it.

GOLF IS MY SOLACE AND ENJOYMENT

Just before the walls came crashing down and I was served with papers from the courts telling me my 3,200 square foot home I had built three-and-a-half years prior was in foreclosure, I had become hooked on playing golf on the Wii Sports video game. I am still intrigued to this day how something as simple as playing Wii Sports golf would reveal to me the next chapter in my life. By having golf and the genuine support of family and friends, I was able to get through that difficult time in my life.

When I first took up golf, I learned quickly that patience was a huge aspect of learning the game. I also had to be patient with myself to get through that difficult period. More importantly, I could not rush the journey; I literally had to learn to be patient with life's lessons and wait to see what the Lord had in store for me. All the while I was taking *action* to improve my situation. Golf started out as a hobby, then one day I said to myself, *Self! Maybe you can apply for a position working at a golf course just to make some extra money*. And that's what I pursued.

INSPIRING OTHERS IS A GIFT OF SURVIVAL

Another remarkable thing happened as a result of my unfortunate set back. For the past 11 years I've shared weekly prayer Scriptures and words of inspiration with a group of 200 people via email. This list that I accumulated over the years includes friends, family, and people from my professional network. This weekly activity was therapeutic for me and became a way for me to cope with what I was dealing with at the time. Before I knew it, I had a following. I wanted to share with others what helped me, on a daily basis, to remain positive and hopeful that my situation would soon change, and maybe theirs would also. I knew for certain my situation was a temporary setback and a greater blessing was waiting for me in the universe. God was not done with me yet.

I am an optimist by nature. The glass is *always* half full. So, for me, a pity party was out of the question. Incessant television watching and sleeping all hours of the day like some people do when depressed was not part of my plan. I am grateful I had a support group (my family) and I sought out positive and successful people who inspired me. I made sure I kept them as my inner circle. I deemed the occasional periods of feeling sorry for myself as normal. It was healthy to recognize my feelings, but I refused to wallow or become a victim because of my circumstance. "This is life! You will overcome like you have before no matter the situation," I repeatedly rehearsed. The choices I made were now in the past. What I was going to do to recover was the real focus. Although the real estate market was in shambles, I still sold a few houses here and there, but I no longer had an interest in remaining in the mortgage industry. So, I picked up a couple of part-time jobs to take care of myself while living with family.

LIVE OUT YOUR PASSION

It wasn't until I started working at the golf course that I really became more passionate about the game of golf. Initially, it was just a way to make some extra income. Unbeknownst to me, it would be the start of my new professional journey.

When in search of a career, my suggestion is to take a moment and write down everything you enjoy doing, even if it sounds silly. Next, take a hard look at that list and you will discover that what you enjoy doing for fun, or as a hobby or something you really are passionate about, could possibly be what you decide to do in life. I strongly believe that all of us possess a talent, skill, or passion that can be turned into a career or business. Mine had been both real estate and mortgages... now golf. I consider myself a serial entrepreneur. Any career I felt passionate about, I later pursued as a separate business for myself.

WHO DO YOU TRUST?

One of the life skills that helped to shape me into the person I am today is *perseverance*. Giving up has never been an option for me, no matter the circumstance. If you were to meet anyone in my family or circle of influence, they would certainly tell you that I have confidence in myself. I am driven, resilient, and fearless, and I never give up on pursuing my dreams. I am always smiling, positive, and encouraging.

My advice to anyone struggling with fear is to surround yourself with people that really believe in you and your vision. Some people rely on others telling them everything they want to hear or on social media to validate who they are or wish to be. I say your true cheerleaders are those that know you personally and have witnessed your struggle and dreams in action. Make a list of friends from your past, new friends, and anyone you trust to encourage you to stay on course... no pun intended.

It's extremely easy to feel like you are on an island. But the reality is that, we are not on this planet just for our own benefit nor are we here to carry the world on our shoulders. We are here to help each other along the way.

Attending worship service definitely played a significant role in my life. I have always been a believer and I feel as though prayer and meditation contributed to my positive state of mind. Knowing and believing in a higher power kept me grounded and safe. Sometimes even when situations didn't always appear in my favor, I believe God had a way of giving me direction and guiding my steps.

I do wish I had been more receptive to consulting a mentor during my real estate journey. Reading books and attending seminars is not enough. Having a mentor or someone I trust to assist me in making realistic decisions without shedding negativity on my ideas or thoughts of success would have been helpful. But also, someone to help keep me accountable for my actions is equally important. I will let you in on a little secret... it *was* recommended that I not purchase this 3,200 square foot home. But, I did it anyway. Sound advice is sometimes hard to hear when you want something so badly.

THE HEALING BEGINS

One of my favorite activities I continued with during the time I was living back with family was exercise. I no longer had my gym membership, so I did the next best thing and exercised at home. I went for runs on the lakefront and I purchased dumbbells and other exercise equipment to keep myself in physical and mental shape. You see, I was not going to stay in a place of despair and feeling sorry for myself. Yes, I made some poor financial decisions, I wasn't prepared for the worst, and I was downsized from my job. I was faced with adversity at every turn, but that didn't mean that my life was over. Praying, meditating, journaling, creating vision boards, exercising, laughing, and playing golf saved me from a deep hole of depression while I figured things out. And so, the healing began. My family played a major role in being there for me as well. I just needed to feel like I was in a safe place and not alone. And I wasn't alone. Thousands of people lost their careers, homes, and relationships and had no one to turn to . . . I was fortunate. The economy had become a global nightmare, which was truly unfortunate. But now I didn't feel so bad.

Let's talk about meditation for a moment. **What is meditation?** Wikipedia defines meditation as "a practice where an individual uses a technique – such as mindfulness, or focusing the mind on a particular object, thought or activity – to train attention and awareness, and achieve a mentally clear and emotionally calm and stable state." Prayer and meditation became an active practice to help me to stay positive and motivated to better my situation until I figured out my next steps on life's journey. I asked myself if remaining in the real estate industry was still an option. If not, what would be my next professional conquest? Working at the golf course was a source of income to take care of myself; I didn't realize that it was my next move. When no one believed golf would pan out to be much of anything, I now had the choice to take what had become my favorite pastime to the next level.

AGE IS NOTHING BUT A NUMBER

In order to move ahead, I needed to get past my issue with age. That was the most difficult part of my transition. I somewhat feared being judged by my peers. But not for very long. Golf had become something I enjoyed, but it was also a way to escape from the fact that I was financially ruined and living back home with Mommy as a grown woman (which in retrospect turned out to be a blessing for us all). We became closer as a family and the continuous laughter was healing for the soul. The book, *Great At Any Age* by Gift Books from Hallmark, helped me to realize I can do anything I set my mind to do no matter how old I am. I just needed to be patient. Attending church, meditating, playing golf, and spending time with family and friends was the best medicine to get me through that difficult period in my life. You wouldn't have known just by looking at me that I was struggling. Yes, my activities had become limited. I couldn't hang out as much. Shopping, traveling, and all the things I had grown to enjoy were reduced drastically. So, I just learned to enjoy the little things like spending time with family, occasional outings with friends that were less costly, and GOLF! Golf had become my passion, my escape into all things wonderful with the world. I never in a million years thought golfing for two to four hours would feel so amazing. Luckily, I was fortunate to work at the golf course so access was plentiful and not expensive for me when I had the time to play. God and golf saved me.

What is most intriguing and inspiring about this part of my story is that I found my passion for golf late in life. Most people, including myself at that time, tend to think that once we arrive at a certain age it's too late to start something new and be really good at it. Well, I am here to tell you that is not true. I played and practiced often during my spare time. Many thought I had played golf in college or maybe in high school. I am fascinated when I hear stories of men and women retiring early from a long, unhappy career or just quitting their profession all together to explore their passions in life... well beyond their 40's and 50's.

I have been known to take my passions and turn them into a business and so can you. I did so with real estate. I had my own property management business for several years.

VICTORY IS ON MY SIDE

I state in my bio that golf was an impetus for the many opportunities that followed. Becoming a high school golf coach, starting a ladies golf league, and inspiring young children and adults to learn the game is worth celebrating. Doing what I love is the best part of this story. I am living the dream. So much so that I was recognized recently by the women of

Zeta Phi Beta Sorority, Inc., Xi Mu Zeta Chapter, as a phenomenal woman. A client was inspired by my story and appreciated the golf lessons. I am grateful for the recognition and hope my story inspires others to take a leap of faith and face fear with courage and determination.

My Journey to Becoming Soul Satisfied

Joyce Dawkins

Here it is 2019 and I am living my best life and doing everything that makes my soul satisfied. I have a successful organization: She ROCKS It. I have a few degrees and certifications. I have several amazing social media platforms: My Soul Point of View, I AM SHE Group, and My Soulfood Point of View. I have several successful event lines: Celebrating Women Who ROCK, The Girlfriend Gathering, and The She Lounge Experience. I belong to one of the best sororities in the world (DST). I am hosting events that engage hundreds of women from across the US each year. I am coaching women on how to live their best life. I am traveling. I have a beautiful family, a dog, and a nice home. I have appeared on television, had several magazine articles written about the work I do, and I have received awards from organizations that honored me for the work I do in the lives of women. My affirmation to myself has been, "I believe I can, so I will." I spoke life into the life I wanted to live and now I'm living my best life.

Yes, all of the above sounds so amazing. It sounds like I have it all. It sounds like my life and my journey have been easy, breezy. Well, that's not true! The journey to getting here was a 27-year journey. Yes, it took 27 years for me to become soul satisfied. So, how did I get here? Let me share My Life, My Test, and My Lesson then end with My Advice to You.

MY LIFE

Twenty-seven years ago, I was in my second year at an HBCU (Historically Black College and University) in Texas. I was hanging on the yard, partying, going to games, cheering for the team, watching the Greeks step, meeting new friends, and just having an amazing college experience. My grades were great, and it was the experience I had heard all about growing up. But after two years, I made a decision that would change my life forever.

I made the decision to go home and transfer to a local state university. It was my choice (and might I add, it was against my parents' wishes). My decision was based on me thinking about their sacrifice of paying cash for me to go to college. And with my younger sister preparing to go into a private high school, I wanted to ease the financial cost for them. Although they never once made an issue about paying out-of-pocket for my education, I just wanted to cut the expense for them. So, I returned home, enrolled in a university, and decided to get a part-time job just to put cash in my pockets while attending school. My parents were totally against me working and going to school; they wanted me to focus totally on college, especially since the school I would be attending was very demanding academically. But, I made my own decision yet again and I began working part-time and going to school full-time.

I wasn't even on the job for four months before the director called me into her office, complimented my work ethic and how professional I was, and presented me with the question: "Would you be interested in a full-time position?" Before thinking about my education and what my parents wanted me to do, I immediately said yes! I saw dollar signs, nothing else. I convinced myself it was a good idea. I kept telling myself, *It's your life and you can do both school and work.* You guessed it, that part-time job would soon become full-time and school turned into not going to school at all.

The career road was one I didn't have planned for myself. My educational dream was to finish college, become a school teacher, and ultimately become a college professor. I had even taken the state exam for educators just to see how I would do, and I passed it on the first try. I was accepted into a fellowship program to teach in the inner city, but I kept working that job and not looking back at what I was walking away from.

Deep down inside, I always wanted to do many things as it related to me being in college. I wanted to finish my education and I always wondered what would have been had I stayed the course? I wanted to be a part of the most amazing sorority, but without being in college or having completed college that wouldn't be possible. With me working full-time, it was almost impossible to reverse my decision and go back to school. However, I always wanted to go back to school and complete the education that I started. I chose another path that would teach me a life lesson I will never forget. Work was going amazing and by my third year on the job, I was given the opportunity to work for another company. I said yes, again looking at the money and never thinking about that education I was once on track to getting. I had purchased my first property, lived there for a few years, then flipped it before "flipping" was a hot topic. I was in the process of building my first home and I had given birth to my second child. Things were going well, but then the unthinkable and the unplanned happened. I was laid off and I was unprepared!

When I was told I was being laid off, all kinds of thoughts ran through my mind. I was now in a place I had never been in as an adult—unemployed. The day they pulled me into the office and said that I was being let go, I began thinking, *Now I have the time I desire but this is not exactly how I thought I would get it.* See, early on after having my second child, postpartum hit. I remember praying and telling God I wanted to be home with my baby, but I knew I also needed to make money to maintain the life I'd built. I didn't think my prayer would grant me my wish by way of losing my job. Then I thought about it. I had also prayed and told God I wanted to finish college, I had a desire to do more in the community, I still had a dream of becoming a member of that sorority, and I wanted more time with my children. I realized I wanted so much but didn't think about what I would have to give up in order to have all of those things. I began to wonder what would happen next after losing my job. So many thoughts were circling around in my mind: *What about money, what about the house, what will people say?*

MY TEST

I arrived home after being laid off and then the unthinkable happened. 24 hours hadn't even passed before I was given the opportunity to go back to work—the same job, same position, and same pay. I was in immediate shock as I had already shared with my family that I was laid off. I had already cleared my desk, said my goodbye's, and prepared myself to write that job off as a part of my journey. I was speechless to say the least, so I asked if I could have 24 hours to give them an answer. I knew that this was something that required a lot of prayer. Getting that call was truly about to test my faith!

See, I had a strong desire to be home with my kids, which I had previously prayed for. I had a desire to complete my education, join that sorority, and become more involved in my community, as well as create an organization to empower women. Those were things I really wanted, but that job prevented me from accomplishing them. So, I questioned myself. Would I say yes immediately and return to the job because of fear, lack of faith, and feeling like a failure? Or would I step out on faith, lose the fear, and know that failure is not an option? I had a choice to make and rather than get on the phone and seek advice from a lot of friends, I decided to speak with one friend and his words were, "Pray about it overnight. Ask God to give you peace about what you should do. If you wake up tomorrow morning still confused and full of worry, doubt, and fear, return to the job because you are not ready to receive what God has planned for you. But if you wake up feeling different, feeling free, you're not confused, and you have a peace that surpasses your understanding, don't return to the place you previously asked God to remove you from. Know that this is Him preparing you to receive the desires of your heart."

When the morning came and I had the call, I chose to say, "No thank you. The job is no longer mine." They couldn't believe it and wouldn't accept my no as an answer, so much so that they called back twice asking again and my response was still no. I said no to the job, no explanation needed, no need to worry, no need to tell others, and no reason to look back. I knew my no would be the answer to my testimony one day. I wasn't sure what would happen next, but I was assured that God's plan for me was far greater than what I had planned for myself at that very moment.

That was the ultimate test of my faith. I never shared with anyone that I received a call back because I didn't want their fear, lack of faith, worry, and advice to cloud what I knew could only be answered by God. I knew if I wanted to hear from God, I could only do so without distractions from others. Although my family would have accepted whatever decision I made, I know they would have looked at it from a perspective of "you have been given a blessing by getting your job back," however they didn't know about the past conversations I had with God asking for this opportunity.

The loss of my job allowed me to be home with my daughter; treat my postpartum; and heal myself mentally, physically, and spiritually. The loss of my job allowed me to return to college to get three degrees and a certification. The loss of my job allowed me to become a member of that sorority I had dreamt about since I was 12 years old. The loss of my job allowed me to serve in the community and mentor others. The loss of my job allowed me to begin to see my purpose in life. The loss of my job allowed me to see my faith work in a way I had never seen it work before in my life.

The loss of my job was God's way of testing me to see if I trusted Him and had enough faith to depend on Him and step out and do the things I had a desire to do for years, like complete my college education and spend more time with my children. Or was I going to be so fearful that I would return back to the place He had just released me from? I tell others to exercise their faith when they are faced with situations they know only God can bring them out of.

MY LESSON

My decision to go against my parents' wishes and work full-time rather than continue full-time in college took me on a journey that started when I was 17 years old and ended when I completed my last degree at 44 years old. What could have taken me a total of four years took me twenty-seven years to accomplish. Do I regret it? At first, I wondered what I had gotten myself into. But when I began to see that my salary was more than the salary of the profession I was in school for, I kind of let that convince me that I had made the right choice. Looking back, I'm not sure if I would have changed anything because my life was fun, exciting, and I learned so much more than what I could have learned in college at the time. I got a life lesson that I would eventually use in the future. Had I not taken the route I took, I wouldn't have this testimony of faith.

The lesson I learned was that the choices you make will ultimately create the chapters in your book of life. I tell others, "Choose your own path on this journey because following the path of someone else can lead you to a place you have no desire to go. Think about the end result of the decisions you make, who they will impact, and ask yourself, 'Will these decisions make me happy?'" In life you will have many tests, how you respond to them will impact you one way or another. You have to know that a test creates a testimony. Trust the process and keep Proverbs 3:5-6 in your heart—"Trust in the Lord with all thine heart; and lean not unto thine own understanding. In all thy ways acknowledge him, and he shall direct thy paths."

MY ADVICE TO YOU

Do the things that make your soul satisfied. Live life the best way you can. Do everything that makes you happy. Don't ask for permission; there is no permission required to be who you desire to be in life. Strive to reach your goals and if you miss the first time, reach out further. Dream big; don't put limitations on where you can go in this life. Be a visionary; whatever you see and want, go after it. Be inspired to inspire someone else. Be empowered to empower someone else. Be motivated to motivate someone else. Use your story to change the life of someone else. My journey took 27 years and you see what happened. I am sharing my journey with you in hopes of inspiring, empowering, and motivating you. It's never too late. No matter how long the journey took and how old you are, you still have right now to begin!

Figuring Out Family First, One Day at a Time

Kathleen Quinn

Purpose... what is purpose and what is my purpose? The definition of purpose is "the reason for which something is done or why something exists." Applying that definition to myself made me think about what my reason is for doing what I do, and even bigger... what am I here to create with my time, talents, and energy?

For me, my purpose is to align my life activities with what is best for my family, my husband, my two children, my parents, my siblings, my large extended family, and my in-laws. As I sat down to write about my journey to living in my purpose, I immediately thought about two things. This first purpose I thought about was when I was seven and contemplated becoming a nun. The second occurred during an exit interview from my first job out of graduate school. I was in the process of leaving a large public accounting firm and was asked why I was leaving. And while I am sure that I gave them some professional reasons, what I recall telling them is, "I want to get married, have kids, and keep working, and I don't see anyone at this firm doing those things successfully." There were no senior women who were married with kids. None. And that was in 1991. I was not in a relationship and could not tell you why or how those words came out of my mouth just then. But I'm glad they came out because as a result, I acknowledged what I wanted in my life. I was almost 30, very single, and envisioning a future that I had no idea how to make a reality. And then it happened, one step at a time, until almost 30 years later here I am with a great career, a long marriage, and two kids. It was never easy. It was never clear where all of this was headed as it happened. I realized after the birth of our first child that my life needed to have a different, clearer, more intentional focus.

I had my first baby at 37 and asked my employer if I could come back to work on a flexible schedule as I had some complications in delivery and was not 100 percent at twelve weeks. And how did they tell me their answer? It was a registered, return receipt letter letting me go via mail with no discussion beyond one conversation that I had with the

CFO. Nothing was said to me about losing my job as a result of my request. I was devastated, panicked, and I did not know what to do. This is where a big family comes in. My cousin's husband called and said he knew someone looking for part-time senior level accounting and finance help. The position was walking distance from my house, and he wanted to know if I was interested. And so, the first big pivot in my career happened. I stopped working for big companies and I went to work for a startup. Did I know what a startup was then? Not at all.

Should I have done some more homework? Absolutely. However, the lead came through my most trusted network of all, they were offering part-time work, and I could walk to work and come home to feed my baby at lunchtime. That was all I needed to know. So, I took the job that changed my life. I never went back to a big company again and for 20 years I have largely avoided being locked into a full-time, inflexible position. Has it been easy? Absolutely not. Was it the right thing for me to do? Absolutely. It became my single purpose to contribute meaningfully in my professional role while having the flexibility to be with my kids when things came up (like the fun stuff of school day events and walking them to school and the not so fun stuff of sick kids, snow days, and cancelled childcare).

Back to the startup. It was in round one of tech booms in 1999–2001 and closed not long after 9/11. The company took the site down, paid off the bills, and everyone was forced to go on new paths. Except, the economy was in the tank in early 2002 and I found out I was pregnant with our second child. Unemployment helped pay bills and again I was panicked and did not know what to do. That was where my network came in. I called my director from the startup, told her I was pregnant and still looking for a job, and I asked her if she had any ideas. She did, and I took my first consulting role doing part-time work for a big company. It was hard being back at a big company, but I was consulting part-time until I had the baby. My director knew me and my capabilities, and we all made it work. How was that possible? It only happened because I had cultivated a network for years and began reaching out, being specific, being flexible, and taking a risk.

I had some fails along the way as well. In spring 2003, I went back to work after baby number two, again in a bad economy, but I was committed to part-time and flexibility. The best I could find was a full-time job with the ability to work from home at least once a week. Other than that, it was a bust. I needed a job to both make money and to stay active in the workforce (which was becoming increasingly challenging with two kids not yet school age, childcare costs, commuting, and my husband's career commitments). When the world wonders why women stop working, the reasons are complex, and everyone's story is different. I was able to work because my husband's employer kicked in with flexibility, my parents and mother-in-law stepped in to fill childcare gaps, and we hired the best childcare person we could. Those things were incredibly expensive, emotionally draining, and complicated to pull off, but the good news was that I had a job. The bad news was that I had a manager who signed up for my arrangement but did not like it and the work was not at all what I expected. My job search for the next right opportunity started within 90 days and I lasted eight months and happily found something new. What didn't work at the big company? One, my manager who knowingly hired me with the work-from-home option had not managed this type of set up before and struggled with trusting me as a new hire. Two, I should have done more homework on the job. What I thought was a financially oriented job turned out to be a compliance job that ended up being filled by a paralegal.

Somewhere along the line during that time period, I did wonder why I was so intent on working. We probably could have made it on one salary. But, that thought made me nervous as I recall the stories of my mom's family. Her dad died at thirty-seven leaving eight kids under twelve and a thirty-four-year-old widow with no work skills. My mother struggled financially her whole life. My mother made very sure that her three daughters would not have those worries and pushed us hard to go into fields where employment was steady. Two of us work in finance and one is a lawyer. Interestingly, my sister-in-law has also worked steadily since graduate school and my brother has been supportive of that. It must run in the family.

Okay, back to getting back to work. Yet again, I was starting over. In late 2003 and early 2004 the economy was not much better. This time I figured out a few things. Remote work was just emerging as a trend, so I focused on finding something close to our home. Since it looked like full-time options were the only ones coming up, I focused hard on money and paid time off in my negotiations and was successful. Negotiating for flexible roles was a lesson in being strategic as I wanted to get the role without giving too much money and power away. I had huge reservations about the traditional culture of this organization. All of the leaders were men with stay at home wives. I traded that off with proximity to home and the ability to control my travel schedule. I thought that after a few years with both kids in elementary school things would get easier. However, I was wrong. As our kids got older, we had more conflicts with before school opportunities, and after school and evening events. Plus, no one ever told me how many days off school kids get now. Between events, days off, sick days, snow days, etc., there was just not enough flexibility and time to make it work and our stress levels rose again. Then one day I thought my husband was in town, but he was in Salt Lake City. That was it. Something had to change because I was overtired, stressed, etc.

I had pitched a 30-hour work week schedule several times previously and was denied. At this point, I thought I had enough successes and a more detailed plan that aligned with other organizational changes going on. We agreed to 30 hours (mostly in the office) and my salary, vacation, bonus, etc., was pro-rated fairly and I retained my benefits. Victory! It was long and hard won and I was so relieved. That setup worked for about six years until a change in leadership occurred and for a whole bunch of reasons it was time to leave. Then, the new leader insisted on full-time in the office and I declined that offer of employment. (Side note: It's always good to have a network that includes labor lawyers who will provide free advice!) What made that a particularly bitter pill to swallow was that the leader making the change was another working mom who had a flexible arrangement for as long as she needed one. The hypocrisy was stunning, and I swore to never treat another person like that no matter what the business needed.

I intentionally cultivated and maintained a large network of accounting and finance professionals with whom I connected personally and professionally. It was important for me to have a network with whom I could be transparent about my life goals and purpose. Two years before those changes went down, I met Deb, the woman who to this day is my mentor and champion. Coincidentally, we had attended the same all-girls high school and when she posted that she was looking for part-time CFOs to join her newly formed consulting firm, I sent a note explaining what my goal was and used our common high school connection to close out the note. We met for coffee and stayed in touch for the next two years. While I spent four months transitioning out of my role, I reconnected with Deb and the stars aligned that my last day at my old company would also be the first day with her consulting firm. It sounds like a dumb idea, but it was great. I worked until 12, went home and had a PB&J sandwich, then headed out to my first meeting as a consulting CFO. I kept waiting for the day that I would miss my old job where I had a corner office, a view of my hometown, and I was only a mile from our house. But, in all honesty, I never missed it for one minute. Why is that? It was no longer a part of my purpose in life and it had become a harmful pull of time and energy. At last, after working for twenty-six years, I was able to pursue my purpose with transparency and clarity.

Sharing my story has given me the gift of reflecting and gaining perspective. First, choose people to be in your life who support your purpose. To be fair, I was born into a great family of parents, siblings, and grandparents with a whole bunch of aunts, uncles, and cousins who have my back. The most important choice I made was my husband. We make it work one day at a time.

Of huge importance has been the women in my personal and professional networks, including those I am connected to virtually. They keep me going. They support me. They provide advice and counsel.

They make introductions. They make me laugh. They make me think. They value me for who I am and for what I share with them.

When I started a career in finance, in a very traditional way, in what seems like a million years ago and in a different lifetime, I never envisioned the life I have now. I had to step out of what everyone expected me to do and step into what I wanted to do with purpose and intention. It did not happen all at once. It happened one day at a time, one choice at a time, and with consistent intention to put my family first. I may not end up with the biggest bank account or the most prestigious role, but I don't care. I am ending up with the life I wanted and the family I fought for one day at a time.

Trust God, Even When
He Changes Your Plans

LaTonya Forrest

My name is LaTonya Forrest. I am currently employed in the field of public service, working with individuals with disabilities and managing cases in a home services program. I am passionate about helping others and encouraging others to walk in their purpose.

As children, we all had dreams of what we hoped to become when we grew up. However, as we grow and progress through life and have different encounters, that dream, vision, or career choice may change. As a child, I often said I wanted to become a nurse. In my mind, I really wanted to be a nurse. I wanted to save people's lives. Every time someone asked me, "What do you want to be when you grow up?" my response was, "A nurse." That is, until I saw an actual operation being performed on television. A man was having gum removed from his stomach because he had swallowed too much of it. When I saw all that blood, I nearly passed out. I could hardly watch the procedure. The very sight of so much blood made me cringe. From that day on, I knew I did not want to become a nurse. However, I still had a passion to help others.

Around the time that I was in the third grade, I decided that I wanted to become a computer programmer. I can honestly say that career choice was not driven by passion but by money; computer programmers make a lot of it. Who wouldn't want to be comfortable, well off, want for nothing, or simply have enough money to survive? However, once I realized all the hard work that really went into coding or computer programming, that was the end of that career goal. I still liked the idea of having a lot of money though.

In high school, I majored in both business and music. I played many sports, but my favorite was volleyball. I was an honor student and also a member of the academic decathlon team. I also worked two to three jobs throughout high school. All of that sounds great, but there was another side to me. I was a rebellious teen. During my sophomore year of high school, I began to date a guy that was in college. By the summer before my senior year of high school, I was pregnant with my first child. My plans changed. Instead of preparing to leave the state for college, hopefully with a volleyball scholarship, I was now preparing to be a mother while completing my high school diploma. I was devastated, but I knew I had to keep going. Quitting was not an option. I had messed up and I had to accept the consequences of my decisions. I had my first child in late March and was graduating in June of 1998. I had to get up early in the morning, take the bus to drop my child off at the day care, then take the bus to school. After school, I had to take the bus to work, then take the bus back to day care to pick up my child, then go home. It wasn't easy.

By the time I made it to college, I had changed my career choice again. This time I wanted to become an accountant. Accountants made pretty good money. I like having money. However, when I went to community college, I did not major in accounting. Because I wanted most of my credits to transfer over to a university, I decided to major in general business. I was able to take accounting 1 and 2. Accounting was very challenging. Although I really loved math, I only averaged a "C" in my accounting courses. That discouraged me from pursuing a degree and career in accounting. Though many years have passed, deep down inside I somehow still have a passion and a love for accounting and may decide to take some accounting courses on a master's level to further my career.

By the time my oldest son turned five, I was pregnant with my second child. I had lost my job shortly after 9/11 and was living off of a severance package and some savings. My children's father was now gone. So, there I was struggling as a single parent trying to finish school. I eventually dropped out of college.

By the time my second child turned five months old, I was involved in another relationship which turned out to be abusive both verbally and physically and resulted in two more children. After five years off and on of looking for change, looking for better, and praying for a better day, I was done. No more. I had a daughter and I was not going to allow my daughter to watch her mother being verbally and physically abused, neither did I want my sons to think it was ok for a man to hit or beat on a woman. I deserved better. My children deserved better.

In 2007, I went back to school and completed my bachelor's degree with honors. Education is important to me. I also wanted my children to know by example that no matter what they face in life, they can overcome anything.

Despite all of the education I had, I still struggled with obtaining a well-paying job. Life had become frustrating for me. I couldn't quite understand why I was in a constant struggle. I was a hard worker but just couldn't seem to land that one job or career that would allow me to sufficiently provide for my family. The one thing that remained consistent was my desire to help people. Although I had made a few bad decisions in my life, I couldn't quite understand why I struggled so hard. I was a good person. I loved everybody. But for some reason, I never received the love I had given. Despite what I'd been through, I never let the actions of another person change who I was. After struggling with life issues, poverty, bad relationships, single parenting, and abuse, I knew there had to be a better way. Why weren't things working out for me? Why was I struggling with negative issues? I knew I had to change my direction so I decided that I needed to seek the Lord. Although I was blessed, a lot of the things I had gone through was because of sin and disobedience. So, I began to talk to the Lord and pray about my purpose. I specifically asked the Lord, "Why did you put me on this earth? Why am I going through so much?" As I sought the Lord, He began to reveal to me my true purpose through His Word (the Bible) and through people. The Lord showed me that my life was being used as a sign to people, as the Lord used Ezekiel as a sign to the children of Israel. The children of Israel were a rebellious people, but God loved them and He loves us. The children of Israel were His chosen people. The Lord saw the children of Israel in their mess (sin), cleaned them up, dressed them in His best, and gave them everything they needed. But the children of Israel were never satisfied and desired the things of the world. They also worshipped other gods. For that reason, they suffered. But God promised to bless them if they would stop worshiping idols and worship Him—the true and living God. The children of Israel's blessings and deliverance was directly tied to their obedience. What is God asking you to give up or do in order to obtain the blessing He has for you?

My purpose is directly tied to ministry (serving) in the church. I've had the opportunity to work in various ministries within the church. Back in 2013, I was working for a major retail store as a cashier. The position was very low paying, and the Lord was dealing with me very heavily concerning my call to ministry. I had discontinued my service with the nursing home ministry because I wanted to focus on providing for my family. Many ministers came through my line, spoke a word over my life, and provided encouragement. However, one night a gentleman in line overheard me speaking to my coworker. He never looked up at me, but he spoke to me while completing his transaction. He asked, "You're not making a lot of money here are you?" My response was, "No." His response was, "And you are not going to until you start preaching the Word of God." Shortly thereafter, I returned to the nursing home ministry and in less than a year my income had more than doubled.

I just want to encourage someone. I don't care what mistakes you have made. If God has told you to do a particular thing, do it. Your prosperity lies in your obedience. Every job I have held has either taught me a lesson or equipped me for my next assignment, career move, and next chapter in life, ultimately equipping me to walk in my purpose. God will not move you into a position that you are not ready for. The area in which you struggle and are tried and tested is usually the area in which you are purposed. Trust God, even when His plan does not match yours. Trust God because if He purposed you to do it, He will and already has given you everything you need to fulfill it. Trust God, even when He changes your plans.

If you want to live in true abundance, you must be willing to be obedient to the will of God. Your eyes may be on that well-paying job or that good looking brother or sister, but what does God want you to have? Abundance is not all about wealth. Abundance comes in different forms, such as peace, true love, happiness, and perhaps a beautiful family. Those things are far better than wealth. Often, we can't live a life of abundance because we are busy chasing the wrong thing.

I just want to encourage somebody, anybody. Trust God for your purpose. Trust God in your process. Trust God even when you can't see your way. Trust God when you don't know which way to turn. Everything you have ever been through ties into your purpose.

I want to encourage someone to live on purpose. Walk in your purpose. I don't care what your past looks like. I don't care what you have been through. It doesn't matter how many mistakes you have made. It doesn't matter who tells you that you can't do it or that your dream or goal is not obtainable. Your purpose was put in you from the foundations of the earth. Everything you need to succeed is already in you. Every experience, set back, and lesson was just preparation. You were being equipped to live out your purpose and to live on purpose. You will find that when you truly begin to do what you were created to do, life will be much more satisfying and worth living, and you will be fulfilling a need. Wherever there is a need, there is purpose.

In the beginning of this chapter, I talked to you about all of the career choices I thought I wanted to make. After I had done things my way to no avail, I had to seek the Lord for my true purpose. It wasn't until I began to walk in the path He chose for me that I began to see myself fulfilling my life's purpose.

The Bible tells us in Matthew 6:33 (KJV), "But seek ye first the kingdom of God, and his righteousness; and all these things shall be added unto you." When you begin to seek God for the things He has for you to do, He will provide you with everything you need to fulfill your purpose and give you a life of abundance. I am a purpose driven woman.

Divorce the Struggle:
Overcoming the Fear of Success

Lesley Martinez

Growing up and thriving in the heart of Chicago, Illinois, is no small task for any child, let alone a Black and Mexican girl with an overactive imagination. In fact, it seems like I had every statistical rationale lined up and ready to reinforce my failure from the day I was born. Within the first 17 years of my life, I endured extreme poverty, serial parental separations, domestic violence, drug addition, mental illness, homelessness, failed entrepreneurial pursuits, and many misunderstood matters of the heart. Feelings of inadequacy plagued my thoughts as early as six years old. *I must be a mistake* was a thought that resonated with me early on, and consequently formed my very low self-esteem. The hyper-consciousness of lack and struggle was reinforced daily and formed a core belief system that buried itself deep in my heart, to the point that as an adult,

I unconsciously sabotaged my own financial success. Throughout my adult life, I've had the daunting task of unraveling the toxic thoughts that undermined my purpose and had me wandering.

Thankfully, there were good experiences in my childhood that seemed to intervene and alter my negative life trajectory. One of those experiences was my mother's choice to homeschool me.

From first to sixth grade, I was homeschooled which gave me space and time to uncover my talents and interests, free from bullies and negative group-think. I learned that my superpower was my creative ability to transform my ideas into tangible projects and that I could potentially earn a lot of money by leveraging all of my gifts and talents. This childhood revelation would be the early formation of my entrepreneurial journey, but it was certainly riddled with failure.

One thing was for sure, I became a certified hustlepreneur. A hustlepreneur is someone who knows how to make money but is stuck in a perpetual cycle of money chasing. This is someone who might gain a significant level of cash and success but isn't able to relax and thrive and is often in a perpetual state of putting out financial fires. This hustlepreneur lifestyle describes my mindset for most of my 20's and mid 30's. I hit a wall with my finances because I didn't know how to invest in myself long-term. I knew how to invest short-term to get the job done and gain decent returns, but I failed at growth planning and scaling. I identified with a hustle mentality because it's what I saw my parents do. Hustling hard was a badge of honor and a sign that I had subconsciously married my struggle.

Marrying your struggle happens when you become comfortable with living in stressful situations. Your ability to navigate life's uncertainties becomes your greatest accomplishment. In fact, you're so good at it, you don't know how to live any other way. You are a dynamic problem solver. You're the pinch hitter, the one who people begin to rely upon to save the day. The problem is, when there is no crisis or no problems, you don't know how to live life. This is where many people struggle because they find purpose in the struggle, and when the struggle is no longer there, they lose their sense of self-worth. This can lead to a cycle of self-sabotage, where you create barriers and crises for yourself in order to maintain your unhealthy but familiar comfort levels.

One of my significant signs of self-sabotage was when I dropped out of film school. I was passionate about being a filmmaker, but I struggled with paying for school. In 2000, during my second year of under-graduate at Columbia College Chicago, I determined that I didn't need a bachelor's degree to be a succes-sful filmmaker. Although this is a true statement for many successful people, I used this belief system to undermine the opportunities I had in front of me. I dropped out of school and obsessively worked on my photography, graphic design, and marketing skills. I quickly became a moderately successful workaholic. I refused to acknowledge that life could be easier if I finished my undergraduate degree. I had commit-ted to a hard and scrappy outsider's life because it was an experience I was used to. In 2006, I had a nervous breakdown. My drinking had gotten out of hand and I realized that unless I redefined myself, I was going to die. From that point on, it's been a jour-ney to unpack and reimagine my life as a thriving, child of God who is loved and worthy of substantial investment. Going back to school was the first step in a new understanding of self-investment. Than-kfully, I have gone from college dropout to earning a PhD in community psychology. Now, my life's work is focused on demystifying the entrepreneurial pro-cess for people like myself who have entrepreneurial desires but limiting circumstances and belief systems.

DIVORCING THE STRUGGLE

Acknowledging that you are operating in a cycle of self-sabotage is essential for you to begin to realign and establish a new paradigm of success that will breakthrough any of your current barriers or success ceilings. I encourage you to dig deep and ask yourself:

Am I addicted to a crisis lifestyle? Do I feel bored or unfulfilled if nothing is going wrong? Does my procrastination undermine my progress? Do I need people to need me in order to be satisfied? Do I struggle with investing in my own wellbeing?

If you've answered "yes" to any of these questions, these next steps will help you to divorce the struggle and overcome the fear of success.

The best way to break off a "marriage" with the struggle is to begin a process of realigning and redefining who you are and where your value lies. The low self-esteem mindset from my childhood began to surface and I realized that for me to break through the invisible ceiling of perpetual lack, I had to be willing to divorce my old mindset and reimagine everything about myself.

Digging up the negative, self-sabotaging behavior in your life is going to require you to activate your realignment by moving forward through these action-oriented steps and experiences. Not everyone requires the same level of activation; however, each one of these categories is necessary for supporting your personal growth.

STEP 1: ACTIVATE THE SHIFT USING AFFIRMATIONS.

Speak self-love affirmations and begin to replace negative thoughts that perpetuate low self-esteem with positive ones that confirm your value and worthiness. These self-love affirmations will begin to replace the negative voice in your head that questions your value or drives you to prove your worth. My personal affirmations are based on actual promises found in God's Word (Christian Bible); they lay a foundation of acceptance and purpose so that I can gain strength in divine order and provision.

STEP 2: KEEP A JOURNAL.

Journaling is essential in your process because it allows you to identify thoughts and your core belief systems without judgment. Reading your words allows you to face reality and make a conscious decision to address the thoughts and replace them. This journal is also where you keep track of your decisions and desires so that you can reflect on how far you've come.

STEP 3: FIND YOUR TRIBE.

Having an accountability circle is a huge step in ensuring you don't fall back into old habits. Finding people who have healthy boundaries and are on their own self-investment journey is a great way to fast-track your progress and stay encouraged.

STEP 4: CREATE YOUR SELF-INVESTMENT STRATEGY.

Once you notice you are gaining confidence in who you are and you truly believe that you are worthy of a life that is enjoyable and abundant, it's time to make a strategy articulating exactly what, when, and how you will execute your self-investment. Whether that is investing in education, launching or growing your business, or doing something you've always wanted to do, you need a plan so that you can track and stay accountable to your goals.

Many of the habits you have formed around the addiction to stress and crisis mode must be broken through the reprogramming of your intentional behavior. You can't be the rescuer for everyone you care about. Establish habits of boundary setting and use response scripts so you can be prepared with an answer for people who ask you anyway. Saying "no" will be essential in this phase.

Here are the key components of your self-investment plan:

Validate your idea.
Sometimes all it takes for you to validate your area of self-investment is to identify someone who has done what you want to do. Whether it's finishing a degree or traveling the world and writing, be sure you have a way to see the arch of where you are heading. This will help you stay encouraged and see the vision unfolding.

Research and design a path forward.
Answer these questions: What are the possible outcomes and opportunities that will arise from my self-investment? What are my known barriers and what resources are available to overcome them? What are the prerequisites? Where do I need to be for this self-investment to fully benefit me?

Whatever the answers to these questions are, you will find a solution and make a commitment to move forward. When you remove the option to bail out, you will realize that you have what you need to live a balanced and more dynamic life.

Celebrate your accomplishments.
Because your self-investment is an activation of self-love, you will need to readily acknowledge and celebrate your milestone accomplishments. Don't beat yourself up if it takes longer than expected. The journey of self-investment is really where the quality of life is improved. Tell your story and begin to encourage others to do the same; you'll see that pouring into others through your self-prioritization is better and more satisfying than coming to everyone's rescue.

Pivot.
It is ok to adjust your self-investment plan. Just make sure that you are pivoting but staying on course regardless of external circumstances. Pivot because you have grace for the journey and not because of internal excuses or making room for fear. Keep in mind that you are worthy and deserving of every good thing that comes your way. Investing in and prioritizing your needs are ways to optimize your life and scale your purpose and impact.

STEP 5: SHOW UP FOR YOURSELF.
Do it! Don't just pay for the class, show up. Be your own best friend, client, or mentor. Cheer yourself on, celebrate the milestones, and vocalize your emotions.

OVERCOMING THE "WHAT IFS?"

What if I fail?

So, what if you fail? Keep moving forward, pivot, adjust, and keep on trying. I'm writing this (in full acknowledgement and despite all of my perceived failures) because I've gotten stronger, wiser, and more dynamic because I'm not afraid to fail. Embrace trips and mishaps and mistakes because they're making you a better person.

What if no one approves?

Assume no one will approve and do it anyway. You'll realize that the fear of people having negative things to say is really your thoughts and core belief system at work. Write out the fears and write out your rebuttals. Defend, to yourself, your right to invest in your ideas and goals. Everyone else will see the results eventually, so don't waste any more precious time on this "What if?"

What if I lose money?

You'd more than likely lose that money doing something less meaningful. When you look at what you spend money on, you'll realize that nothing brings a better return on investment like self-investment. Yes, that degree is expensive, but even if it only gets you through one extra door of possibility, you are certainly worth every penny.

Ok, so here we are at my conclusion. You now have a sense of how to identify self-sabotaging behaviors and mindsets. You now also know what strategies to use to begin changing your previous behaviors and you've created your self-investment roadmap that you are committed to seeing through even if you have to pivot and adjust. Once you learn this process for one goal, you will see that you will start to execute it without hesitation for future goals. It will become a way of life and you will be a better, more fulfilled person because of it.

Redefine Your Life by Redefining Success

Liane Williams

It's funny how uncertainty and certainty can show up in the same place at the same time. Often, it's something small like I'm certain I need to get dressed for work, but I'm uncertain about what to wear. And sometimes, it's life changing.

While in high school, I decided to take the train to downtown Chicago with some friends. As the train pulled into the next station, I saw her. The first thing I noticed about her was that she had a commanding presence. The wind blew through her hair and her trench coat opened to reveal a stylish suit. She wore heels, had a briefcase in one hand, and looked as though she knew exactly where she was going. Not just right then, but for the next ten years. In my mind, she was obviously successful. We passed her in only a few seconds, and although I never saw her again, she made a lasting impression on my young mind.

To me, The Lady on the Train was a businesswoman who lived in The Land of Success, and I was certain that I wanted to be her. Of course, I had no idea how to do that, and that's where uncertainty entered.

Over the years, her image stayed with me, as did the questions: What did she do that made her so successful? Did she work for a large company or own her own business? Where did she get that suit? Although I knew I would never learn the answers to many of my questions, I was determined to be just like her.

The first step seemed obvious: go to college. Next, choose a major. If I had any hopes of becoming like The Lady on the Train, I knew I had to be a businesswoman; however, after one year as an "undecided" major, I still hadn't figured out how to get closer to my goal. Two years and two majors later, I finally decided on business administration. I reasoned that it was business related, but still broad enough to be flexible. Looking back, the truth was that I had absolutely no idea what I wanted to do.

Toward the end of my junior year, a friend advised me to apply for an internship with State Farm Insurance to get some exposure to the business world. While uncertain about State Farm, I was certain I needed to work, so I applied and was accepted.

By the end of the program, I was told a job would be waiting for me after graduation. That was certainly good news, but the job wasn't in Chicago. To be The Lady on the Train, I had to get a job in downtown Chicago. I had to take the train to work and have the wind blow through my hair. However, I rationalized that it was a minor detour and that at any time I could move back to Chicago and get back on track.

During my "minor detour," which lasted eleven years, I earned several promotions and a transfer back to Chicago. My path, however, never seemed to bring me any closer to my dream. I was leading a successful life, working for State Farm training the sales force and their teams, when agents began asking me why I had not considered opening my own State Farm office. Sales had not been a career I had ever imagined myself in, and I wasn't sure I could be successful at it. It did not fit my vision of The Lady on the Train, but after a lot of soul searching, I decided to take the plunge.

Fear engulfed me those first months before and after opening my business. The first year was a blur. The night before I opened my business, my boyfriend proposed. Most of the early days were spent making calls alternating between discussing the cost of car insurance and the price of flower arrangements. I missed the joy of planning a wedding and being a newlywed because I was working twelve or more hours a day. Fortunately, my new husband traveled extensively with his job, so he wasn't home to notice how much he would have been ignored in those early days. I was drowning and didn't even realize it.

The business was growing, but I couldn't help noticing how much easier it seemed for my counterparts. We all seemed to be working the same plan, but I didn't seem to be getting the same results. I couldn't understand what I was doing wrong, so I worked harder. This was not what I envisioned when I saw The Lady on the Train. She seemed to have it all under control. What was I missing?

After two and a half years, we discovered we were pregnant with our first child. Although I was happy, I worried constantly about how a baby would fit into our crazy schedules. I was working long hours and my husband was on the road 75 percent of the time. How was I going to do it all? Twenty weeks into my pregnancy, I got the answer, and it wasn't good.

The contractions started late on a Sunday night. Sitting in the emergency room, tears filled my eyes while I was hooked up to a monitor. Had I done something to jeopardize the health of my baby? When the baby was safe, I was told to go directly home, straight to bed, and to stay there until further notice.

While in bed for the next five weeks, I was consumed with guilt. Although the doctors weren't sure that stress played a part in my complications, I was certain I was to blame. Convinced I was doomed to be a terrible mother even before my child was born, I began to slip into a depression. How could I keep both my baby and my business alive? My husband said I was going to have to cut back on my hours and asked me if I was willing to trade the life of our child for my business. It was a real wake up call for me. I had to start to really evaluate what was important to me.

I thought back to a conversation I had years before with a very successful agent. He talked about how his wife took care of everything at home while he built and maintained his business. He spent most of his time in the office, even after he was clearly successful, but implied the sacrifice of not seeing his children grow up was "worth it" because the result was a thriving business and large income to support his family.

Let's face it. Entrepreneurs are in business to make money. I was no different, but I had to ask myself what cost I was willing to pay. Was it going to be "worth it" to work for a great house that I hardly lived in? Was it going to be "worth it" to have money for vacations that I didn't have time to go on? Was it going to be "worth it" to make money to help support a family I hardly spent time with?

I'd like to say that my immediate answer was no, but it wasn't. Although I cut back on my hours once I was "paroled" from my bed rest sentence, I still believed I could have it all. I fell into the Superwoman Syndrome. Every day, I got up and tried to have what I envisioned as the perfect day. My fantasy started with me getting up early, exercising, and heading out to daycare early with my son. While at the office, I would make several sales and would then leave by 5:00 p.m. After picking up my son, I would head home to cook the perfect meal for my husband and spend an evening of quality time with my family. Finally, while my husband put our son to bed, I would slip into some sexy lingerie and, well, end the day as perfectly as it began. Goals!

Of course, this perfect day never happened. I was exhausted, so I overslept, left the house late, struggled with sales, and got home too late to cook. I would spend a little time with my family, but by the time my son was in bed, I was passed out as well. Rise and repeat.

So, after five more years, another pregnancy, another bed rest, and another son, the cracks in my life, and in my mind, started to really appear. No matter where I was or what I was doing, I was plagued with guilt. If I was at home, I felt I was neglecting my business. If I was at work, I felt like I should be spending more time with my family. When I was playing with the children, I felt like I should be paying more attention to my husband. When I was out with my husband, I felt like I wasn't being a good mother. Once again, I slipped into a depression. When my husband finally confessed he was unhappy, I knew I had to make a change. It was now the ONLY thing I was certain of.

He had been begging me to seek counseling, but I had resisted. Superwoman does not need counseling. Superwoman can handle everything! But that was the problem. I was not handling anything. I was failing in every aspect of my life and I couldn't understand why. I am a strong Christian, and I had prayed before making every move in my life. I prayed that God would send me a good husband, and He did. I had prayed that God would direct me about opening a business, and He did. I prayed to God to bless me with two sons, and He did. If He had given all this to me, why was I not able to manage it?

Desperate, I finally agreed to counseling and began to see the root causes of my issues. I had built a life based on completely unrealistic expectations of what success was supposed to look like for me. I had taken a ridiculous high school vision of some woman on a train that I knew nothing about and tried to pattern my life around a fantasy. For all I knew, her life could have been just as big a train wreck as mine was now. I had also been trying to measure up to all the other agents around me. If my numbers weren't as good as the top producers, and they never were, I was devastated. Feelings of inadequacy were devouring me. My counselor urged me to think and pray about what was most important to me. What was God's real desire for me? If I had to let go of something in my life, what would be the hardest thing to live without?

Well, I was certain of the answer. My relationship with God and my family were at the top of the list. But with the answer came the uncertainty of how to make it all work together. I didn't think I was supposed to give up the business, but how could I fit it into a healthier lifestyle? The first thing I had to do was reevaluate my idea of what success looked like. I had based the success of my business on gaining more than someone else, which was my first mistake. So, I decided to rework my business plan based on goals I wanted to achieve that reflected my values, which included a happy family life. I admit that it was difficult to give up some of those dreams, no matter how unrealistic they were. But those dreams didn't make sense for me. Instead of letting my business run me, I had to decide how I wanted to run my business. What was I willing to sacrifice? I knew I wanted to spend more time with my family and on the things that made me feel whole, but how would I manage that?

Limiting my working hours would be key. My business was fully staffed, so I just had to trust that my employees were capable of doing the work I had hired them to do. Then, I worked on setting realistic sales goals for my office. Reflecting on some of the reasons I wanted to go into business in the first place also helped. I wanted to control my own future, provide employment to someone who needed a job, and help support myself (and a family) financially. I also wanted a flexible schedule so that I would be able to do more of the things I loved in my personal life. Once I realized that I could still have all of those things, it changed the way I approached everything. Estimating the income I would need and the sales it would take to maintain that income resulted in a more realistic business plan.

The most important thing I did was to stop evaluating my life based on others. When I took off my Superwoman cape and retired my fantasy about The Lady on the Train, it was like a weight had been lifted off my shoulders. Spending more time with my family and returning to the activities I loved brought joy back into my life. Slowly, I found myself again.

When I look back on those years, I'm grateful. Had I not experienced the fear, anxiety, and depression that caused me to slow down, I might have worked myself into an early grave or out of a happy marriage. For me, finding balance in my life has been the real key to success. The beauty of owning your own business is that you get to determine what success looks like for you. I had to learn the hard way to set a measure of success based on what was right for me and my family, not based on what someone else was doing. As a result, I have successfully been in business for 24 years. I have supported my family, not just financially, but by never missing a spelling bee, a swim meet, or a water polo game. We've had wonderful family vacations, dinners on the patio, and game nights. My husband and I rediscovered date night, have been married for over 23 years, and are now enjoying the next phase of our lives as empty nesters. I've learned to put my family first. So when difficult times have come, and they always do, we have been there to support one another. Now, I also have time to do the things I love to do. I sing on my praise and worship team and with a jazz band, I've been in many community theater productions, and I am a voice over actor. I have found my voice, literally. I may have been uncertain about how my choices would affect me, my business, and my family, but looking back, I'm certain that I made the right ones.

Big Dreams, Bigger Fears: How Can I Survive?

Molly Hebda

"What you have to understand is that when we get in there and you start to bleed, you will die."

That was the first thing the specialist said to me after he sat down. It was 8:00 a.m., I hadn't had any coffee yet, and I failed to ask anyone to come with me to my appointment. My husband was traveling, and I had been to almost every appointment on my own that year. The specialist continued to explain more about the upcoming procedure for my liver, but I barely heard what he was saying.

It was the most terrifying thing anyone has ever said to me. Even more terrifying than when I was living with my boyfriend in college and he had his fingers wrapped around my neck and was telling me that he was going to snap it. My survival instincts kicked in, and I was able to talk my way into leaving that day. I was left physically and emotionally battered and bruised, but I was alive. I had survived.

When I was diagnosed with thyroid cancer, not long after my husband and I got married, my mind went to horrible places at first and then my body did not take well to having my thyroid removed. But, with cancer, you get your diagnosis, and you fight like hell.

This was different. I was devastated. It broke me and collapsed every single wall I had ever built up around myself. I tried hard to cover up my fear with work commitments and staying busy during the month I had to wait for my procedure, but nothing helped to take away my fear. I had absolutely no control over what was about to happen to me, and I didn't know how to handle or accept that.

When I started my photography business during the summer of 2016, I had never even owned a DSLR camera. My photography story didn't start with the usual, "I was practically born with a camera in my hand." Instead, I was working as a virtual assistant and producer for a pole dancing company. A few years prior, I had signed up to take pole dancing classes around the same time I received the diagnosis for my thyroid cancer. Taking those classes and being in such a positive environment, surrounded by supportive women, not only helped my recovery from cancer but it helped me regulate my body and mind afterwards. I went all in with classes and even began teaching. During my first and only competition, I busted my shoulder and could no longer teach. Because my body was not able to fully recover after surgery, I started managing the studio, just so I could continue to be a part of the community. That led to another job working virtually for a studio in Los Angeles. With any position I ever held, I found myself learning on the fly. If I was asked if I knew how to do something, I said, "Sure!" and figured out how to do it afterwards. I built our websites, created marketing, and helped produce full productions in Las Vegas and L.A. Because I was not on location when they had their studio photoshoots, I never quite had the material for the marketing that I wanted to create. After a couple years of struggling and complaining to my husband, he encouraged me to buy a camera and do it myself.

My camera arrived in June and by August I was out in the woods taking pictures of women in cocktail dresses. I had no business being out there with that camera, but the images that popped up on my viewfinder excited me. I was actually able to create the images that were in my head. I moved into my first studio space six months later so that I could venture into boudoir photography. The studio was basically a closet in the basement of a local office building, but it was all mine. I found that I loved helping women find the confidence they never knew they had. After seeing the transformation of my students at the pole studio, this genre of photography seemed like the perfect fit.

Having my own business was a different beast than trying to run someone else's. I had always been the one to support others in making their dreams happen and here I was trying to make these things happen for myself. It was chaos and I was a mess, but I absolutely loved it all.

I never graduated from college. I didn't have the money to complete my last year, and my family didn't have the means to help. They were never good at budgeting or finance. Their idea of paying a bill was paying it once that utility was shut off. It's taken me some time to figure out the financial side of my business and actually take home money to benefit my family. Determined to make it work, I have devoured every business book, found support through online groups, and made connections at workshops in Chicago.

As I began taking photos of women in the woods, I stumbled upon a Facebook group based in Scotland for photographers. They offered weekly photo challenges and the first time I entered I was featured on their blog. They were the most positive group on social media. It was all support, no negativity or competition. After joining, the women who ran the group posed the question, "Who in this group is either in business or thinking of starting a business as a photographer?" Most of us fell within those categories so they created an online photography business training center. Joining gave me a crash course in running my business. As the program grew, smaller accountability groups were created to help us stay on track. My first group quickly folded, but in December 2018, I was asked to join another group that had been going strong since the beginning. These are my people. We talk about life and hardships, trauma, and success. I joined just after surviving my liver procedure, and it's been a blessing to be so raw about my journey and the process to figure out my purpose in life.

In February 2018, just after turning 40 years old, I landed in the ER with shortness of breath and tightness in my chest. I had traveled that weekend so they thought it might have been a blood clot. After staying the night in the hospital and having many scans and tests, I was sent home with a pile of reports to follow up on with my doctor. As I was sitting with my primary care physician, I asked him what the phrase, "scattered glass opacities in the lungs" meant. My imagination brought me to the conclusion that my shortness of breath and the tightness in my chest were due to me having used too much glitter in my photoshoots. Painting women and mermaids with mounds of glitter was kind of my thing. But, he was not so tickled by my humor. He sent me off to a pulmonologist who confirmed I had fluid (thankfully, not glitter) in my lungs.

For the rest of 2018, I saw many specialists. The doctors tried to piece together the main cause for the symptoms that had slowly developed over the past year. I had been so focused on running my business that I had completely lost sight of my health. I was exhausted, I struggled to walk up a flight of stairs without having to catch my breath, and I had gained over 50 pounds since starting my business. I just brushed it off to not working out and eating out more than we had home cooked meals because I was busy. The doctors were determined to figure me out. That was the first time, ever, that I had a team of doctors that were so willing to put in the effort. I had always had weird ailments throughout my life, but most of the time doctors threw up their hands saying they didn't know what was wrong or why I had the problems I came in with. I had learned to deal with the pain and symptoms and move on with my life. This time, my body kept getting worse. If I wanted to have any chance of getting back to taking care of my family and building my business, I had to find out what was wrong.

With each scan, a note kept popping up about a possible malformation in my liver. My gastroenterologist consulted with a radiology specialist to see if we should look into this note further. The specialist was actually excited to meet me. Apparently, this is a rare and exciting diagnosis for these types of doctors. My liver was special.

One of the main veins from my intestines, that is supposed to feed into my liver, had bypassed the liver going straight into the vein that feeds my lungs. This all happened while I was a developing embryo, and when I was younger the technology wasn't as advanced as it is today. Over time, the vein had become enlarged and highly pressurized, putting extra strain on my lungs and heart and feeding my body unfiltered, toxic blood. This could be what had caused my thyroid cancer and why my shoulder never healed properly. Plus, it explained some of the other medical issues including most of my weight gain, fluid in my lungs, constant migraines, memory loss, and most recently the onset of double vision. This specialist wanted to do an experimental procedure to fix the vein, ultimately restoring my body back to a normal state.

At first, I was excited about the possibility of living a normal and healthy life, one that I had never known, but the idea of dying was not one I was ready for. I was warned that if I didn't go through with the procedure, it was just a matter of time before the vein gave out on its own or my heart failed because of the excess pressure. Either way, I could die.

In the movies, the person dying is completely calm and accepting of the imminent death before them. There's a soft, diffused glow of light over their face and they always have something beautiful and wise to say to their loved ones. I, on the other hand, felt like a caged beast trying to escape from the zoo. The night before my procedure, I wanted to write something meaningful to my son, my husband, and my family and friends. When I sat down, I could not write what they had meant to me, how they had impacted my life, or what I wanted for them for their future. I was frozen with fear and my mind was blank. I remember sitting with my notebook and pen in hand and all that I had left on those pages were tear stains and a few doodles. I thought to myself, *If I die*

tomorrow, I will leave them and the world nothing.
I felt defeated and horribly sad. The next morning, I said goodbye to my son before my husband drove him to school. He closed the door and I stood in our kitchen and sobbed. I didn't know if he would come home to having a mom. I was sure I would be missed, but I had just spent the last three years with my head down in my business, hiding from the fact that I was sick and not connecting with my family or friends.

When I woke up from the procedure, I guess I carried my beast mentality and fight into recovery. The specialist said I was swearing like a truck driver and making all of his residents and staff laugh. That was not my day to die.

A year ago, I wasn't making plans past my procedure date. I was taking photos up until the day before, wondering if those people would actually ever get to see their photos. This year, I moved into a new studio. It's enormous compared to that first little studio in the basement and it actually has windows that flood the space with light. I am preparing to paint a glitter wall to showcase a gallery of inspirational client portraits. Time has softened my scars, and even my fight, just as it did after college and cancer. The only evidence left from the procedure is a small, raised red dot on my neck, next to the faded scar where my thyroid had been removed. Being kind to myself as I overcome my past, having the patience to sit amongst the debris in the present moment, and not stressing over the unknown of the future are things I have to remind myself to do every day.

Right before going into my procedure, I helped to create a women's group in town for local women in business. The more women I meet through my business and this group, the more energy and inspiration I gain from their successes. The group is meant to build organic relationships and move us past competition. Discussing not only business but more importantly how to balance work, family, and self-care has helped us all realize that we are not alone. Not surprisingly, each one of us has gone through some kind of trauma in our lives. And although each of our paths are completely different, each of us have had to find similar ways to survive. I continue learning from the online photography group based in Scotland. This coming spring, together with my accountability group, we will fly across the pond to finally meet up in person. Moving forward, I plan on planting seeds instead of rebuilding walls so that by the time I face death again, I won't have to worry about what I'm leaving behind.

A year after my procedure, I don't have it all figured out. I shouldn't expect myself to. My body is still healing and my brain is still processing. But what's amazing is that I am finally giving myself permission to heal. Yes, I continue to have moments when I put my head down and focus on my business, but I also choose to step away from the hustle to make my family, friends, and myself a priority. It's exciting to now look to the future with my husband as we support our son who is ready to go after his college dreams.

Reflecting on how 2018 was the year that broke me, and how I could not even speak about having to face death, I am finding beauty and clarity amongst the pieces. I take each failure as a lesson learned (oh, have I been handed the lessons), not as a defeat. Again, here I am saying, "I survived!" But this time, it comes with the gift of finding my voice and the opportunity to finally live.

The Struggle Is Real ... but Continue to Push!

Muhjah Stewart McCaskill

To push from fear to faith is to understand where fear comes from and change it. This requires patience and perseverance. It's a very simple equation: God first, then trust yourself, and lastly trust the process!

I'm Muhjah. I am a mother, manager, student, business owner, and mentor. When I set my mind to accomplish something, I use everything in me to push through to the finish line. When I tell you that I try to always do my best to complete things, even if delivering later than expected, I DO! My best work is usually produced under some sort of pressure. This may not sound realistic to some, but being put under pressure challenges me and I like it! I know you may ask, "Why does she do that?" My answer? "Because, to me, sometimes NOT finishing a task scares me more." I do way too much all the time! I also can get overwhelmed because I don't know how to say NO. I feel like I can change the world most days! As a matter of fact, I know I can! With that mentality, I put myself under more pressure than necessary because I commit to doing things that realistically I don't have the time to do and I'm scrambling to finish. I'm sometimes too stubborn to let anyone tell me differently. Do I accomplish it all? Absolutely not!

Sometimes I struggle with not being able to accomplish all I have committed to do. In my mind, it helps that I keep sight of the much bigger picture. That bigger picture is to impact as many people as God will allow me to. Now I'm bragging on God! I believe my life is destined by God and because of that belief, I know He has given me all of these wonderful things to do. I believe that He will give me the strength I need to finish strong. Although He shows me all of the things He wants me to do, I am not always clear on the small details. God deals with me in the bigger picture view. For instance, when I heard I was supposed to start a business, I didn't know what kind of business it was. All I knew was that it had something to do with helping kids be creative and keeping them off the streets and safe. I didn't see the small details I needed to start the business or how we would even work with the kids. The steps I needed to take were the pieces I was missing. What

I didn't know was that God was lining me up with school advisors and business people who would help me get to the final result of starting the business and working with the kids. This process took months to accomplish. But, ultimately, the business developed from start-up to strengthening art and writing skills, finally to impacting youth through financial literacy and entrepreneurship. In my mind, business was supposed to happen overnight. But, it took us five years to understand our population and an additional five years to help our students build successful businesses and understand how those businesses can improve the communities they serve.

A friend of mine once said to me "Muhjah, you don't fail well!" That was very surreal. "What do you mean I don't fail well?" I asked. Her response was, "Because everything you put your mind to you accomplish." When I feel like I'm going to fail, I get extremely frustrated and anxious. That is because, like I said before, I feel like God gave ideas and vision to me, so He will give me what I need to see those ideas and visions through. My assignment is to change lives for the better. I own that and I strive for that. When I don't feel like I'm impacting the world the way I think I should, I start working out strategic plans in my mind to get to the place I feel like I should be so that I can complete the part of the task that is missing. I am beginning to understand that things have to happen in God's timing and that I have to get out of the way. So I'm learning how to stop, count to 10, breathe, plan out my tasks, and complete what I can.

In August of 2007, God told me to go back to college. For years, I'd petitioned Him to give me an opportunity to finish and now He was giving me that opportunity. I have ingrained in my children the importance of graduating from college and to not just stop there but go further than I did. Well, I had not even graduated from college, so it was very important that I did. After 20 years, I finished and got my degree in 2014. Not only did I obtain my degree, but I graduated with honors, was inducted into an international business honors society, and I received a scholarship my senior year. Back to God telling me to go back to college. When He told me to go back, I didn't understand how I was supposed to do that. I was working second shift on my job at a prison as an officer, I had recently gotten married, and I had a new baby and three smaller children under the age of eleven.

For the first time in my life, I could not see the bigger picture. God's timing did not seem right to me. I found all sorts of reasons why I should not go back. God and I had a very blunt conversation in the car about that issue one morning on my way to work. As any curious child would ask their parent, I questioned God. All I heard Him say was, "Go back to school." I didn't understand what He was doing at the time but I'm so glad I was obedient, otherwise I would not be where I am now!

When God told me to go back to college, I had no idea how or where to start. I wasn't even sure what college to attend. Little did I know, God was setting things in motion. There were so many feelings going on in me at the same time—fear, apprehension, and questioning how to fill the roles I currently had and how to make them work. In August of 2007, I received a call for a promotion. The promotion was for me to leave the prison and move to a different department with the ability to work daytime hours with no overnights or late shifts. I accepted that promotion, then God allowed me to receive another promotion four months later. When I received the call from human resources, I could not believe it. I was still waiting to be certified in my current roll. Human resources advised me that since I was so close to being certified, they would hold the promotion for me. Once I became certified, I was offered the job.

By January 2008, I was in my second promotion in less than a year and well on my way to fulfilling His timeline.

I started my new role as manager with no staff. Three months later, God blessed me with a wonderful team of employees who still, to this day, support me in everything I do. The department had been fighting to get staff for years. Here I came as a new manager and the doors and windows poured out everything I needed to get ready for the new path I was going to travel down. While I was questioning God, I was still being obedient. I didn't understand what He was doing, but I stayed the course. He paved the way with more money, normal hours, and a whole lot of responsibility at work and at home. But I had a good team, so I was able to train them and leave them in charge knowing they would ensure the office ran the way it should if I was not there.

In August of 2008, God said to me, "Ok, it's time to go to school and I want you to go to Chicago State University." I went to the school to register and meet with my now mentor, and he took me under his wing. He sat with me every semester, talked me through the challenges, and showed me how to graduate without destroying myself. I did it, I finished! I attended school at night, on weekends, online, and during the summer and winter breaks. I took my kids to school with me, and I went home at night and helped them with their homework. I also cooked and took care of home. After I finished with my kids, I stayed up and studied. I studied on my lunch breaks too. God blessed me to have favor with management. They allowed me to leave work in the middle of the day to attend classes. They understood that I needed to be at home with my children at night. I wasn't able to schedule my classes every semester during work hours, but when I could, my boss allowed me to be off and it was greatly appreciated!

I didn't miss a beat! I never missed my sons sporting events, my children's piano or chorus recitals, or parent teacher conferences. And I was an active member on my children's local school council. When people ask me how I did it, I tell them I didn't, it was God. He carried me, supported me, sent people to help me, and looked after my mental health so that it wasn't as hard as it seemed.

My first semester back at school in August 2008, I took a business management class. In the class, our assignment was to write a business plan for a business we would like to start. I had no idea what my business would be, so I just wrote a makeshift plan about the park district programming. My professor read the plan and said to me, "You got an A. You won't be presenting this to the class. You're going to actually start this business." I looked at him like he was crazy. At that time, I didn't know God was getting me ready to be a successful manager and business owner. I didn't even fully know what I was going to major in. I never wanted to be a business owner; it never crossed my mind. I just wanted to be a good example to my children about the importance of finishing college. Years later, almost to the date that God told me to go back to school, He birthed a non-profit business out of me. September 10, 2010 was our official certification date.

While working in the male max prison, I was able to see a lot of brilliance, talent, and drive. I never wanted to know the crimes they committed because I wasn't there to judge, I was there to ensure they did not leave the prison and we kept order. I always wondered if they had people or programs that could have potentially steered them into something better than prison. I thought about how the inmates could organize groups of other inmates and keep order. What if they were able to use that same gift in the streets to help make our neighborhoods better? The influence they had on their peers was amazing and scary at the same time. I had to take into consideration where

I worked. How could they run drugs, gangs, security, and product like a business the way they had? If there had been people out there in the world who could have taught them how to take their skills and abilities to build something legitimate and good, would they be in prison?

So, when God challenged me to start the business, He said to me, "You will start with the children who are in third grade. You will give them creative outlets that are not currently in the schools or park districts that will occupy their minds and help them think outside the box of what their normal, everyday circumstances look like. You are going to stop the school to prison pipeline with mentorships and creative programing." I didn't know how I was going to do that, and I did not have a team or a real plan. Little did I know, finishing school was all a part of that plan. Working in the prison was all a part of that plan. Being involved in my children's lives was all a part of that plan. Being a good boss was all a part of that plan. And, finally being a wife was all a part of that plan. What I learned from all of my experiences in life was that perseverance, trust, and having faith in my abilities was more than enough!

Everything we go through in life is designed to put us under extreme pressure so that we can come out shining like the rare stones we are. Pressure is designed to make us strong. Trials don't feel good while we go through them, but the great thing about that is we are not staying there, we are pushing past the obstacles and coming out on the other side. I used to ask God all the time, "Why me? Why do I have to endure so much pain and hardship?" He said to me in his Daddy voice, "Why not you? You are built for the pressure so walk in it." I didn't understand at first, but as I stand here in my truth with tears in my eyes, I can see the lives I have touched, and it is all worth it!

One morning as I was ironing my clothes for work and a friend and I were sharing our struggles, she said, "Girl, this is so crazy all the stuff we have to go through." I heard the Spirit of the Lord say for me to tell her, "It's not crazy, its necessary and it's intentional!" She said "Girl, what did you say?" I said, "It's not crazy, its necessary and it's intentional!" Our lives and the work we do are necessary and intentional!

When you feel like you can't take any more, it's ok to say you're tired, but don't give up. It's ok to be weary, but don't fall. And it's ok to not understand. Just know that the plans are being laid out before you, you just may not see them yet. As God carried the man through the sand and all he could see was one set of footprints, know that God is also carrying you. You are not alone in any facet of your life, just look to the circle of support God has given you. Begin to assess the strengths and weaknesses of that circle. Know those who are there for a reason and those who are there for a season. Meet people where they are and love them anyway. Some are there to help you grow and get to the finish line. Some are there to be a distraction. When you're unsure of the path or the people, don't be afraid to ask God.

Had I not trusted myself enough to know I was worthy of the things God has for me, I would not be here today doing the work He has called me to do! Had I not trusted and pushed past fear without knowing what was on the other side, I couldn't be who I am today, and lives could not have been changed. I often think to myself and wonder, as I did when I worked in the prison, what my life would be like had I not listened to God or trusted in myself. Could I be where I am today? I'm glad that I listened and was obedient! You can do anything you set your mind to. All it takes is a little trust in yourself, a teaspoon of faith, a cup of perseverance, hearing God's strategy, and trusting Him!

The 3 Ps to Success: Purpose, Plan, and Preparation

Sandy Sanders

"In any moment of decision,
the best thing you can do is the right thing,
the next best thing is the wrong thing,
and the worst thing you can do is nothing."
—Theodore Roosevelt

A change can only come after you are fed up with your current state of being and make the decision to do something different. If you don't decide, you are technically making the decision to do nothing. You must start with the decision to take action!

I didn't know exactly when it happened until I looked back in my journal. My turning point was in the early morning hours of January 15, 2013. That was the day that my life would monumentally change. I knew that if I wanted to accelerate the accomplishment of my goals, I had to unlock the secret to success. It was that morning during my meditation that the answer came in three words—**Purpose, Plan, and Preparation**! I made the decision to clearly define my purpose, create a well laid out plan, and prepare to step into my destiny.

Although I have always been very driven with high expectations of myself, I seemed to have hit a limit of achievement. I possessed the desire to go to the next level, but instead of a clearly defined purpose, I had a vague vision of success. What I realized was that I had not hit the point where that desire was strong enough to remove the apathy from my life. I had no clue that apathy was the stumbling block preventing me from moving forward. I was truly indifferent, as my desire or vision of the next level wasn't strong enough, and subconsciously I had a feeling of helplessness. I wasn't driven by either inspiration or desperation. What was stopping me? What was my roadblock? I realized it was that dreaded four letter word—FEAR!

Fear has a crippling effect. I have always been reminded, "For God has not given us a spirit of fear, but of power and of love and of a sound mind." (2 Timothy 1:7; NKJV). Fear is not empowering, and it prevents your mind from formulating thoughts that will help you thrive and be successful. But what did I fear? Like most people, I feared rejection, making mistakes, and ultimately failure. I realized that I could not allow past rejections or failures to stop me from pursuing my goals and dreams. I needed confidence to combat the fear.

Too many women don't have enough confidence to make bold moves and take risks as it relates to entrepreneurship and their careers. We think we aren't ready; we feel like we are underprepared and unqualified, which ultimately fills us with fear. Men don't have that problem. They don't feel the need to have it all worked out before making a move. If they have it partially worked out, that's good enough for them. A *Harvard Business Review* article entitled "Why Women Don't Apply for Jobs Unless They're 100% Qualified" validates some of the reasons. We need to take a lesson out of their book and get out of our head! We disrupt our own success by undervaluing ourselves, not asking for help or directions, being afraid of self-promotion, or not making relationships a priority.

Napoleon Hill said, "Whatever the mind can conceive and believe, it can achieve." You will accomplish anything you set out to do with all your heart, soul, and mind. However, that will require you to first make the **decision to ACT** upon the **three P's—Purpose, Plan, Preparation**, remove apathy from your life, and confidently face your fears! You can't decide to do NO-thing.

THE SECRET IS IN THE ACTION

We all know that knowledge and understanding will yield success. You've heard the phrase "knowledge is power," but is it enough to just possess knowledge? No, it is applied knowledge that ignites change. Taking action is the only way to succeed. Your value and success will be determined by your ability to act and follow instructions. Success is a journey that must be navigated. Think of it as taking a road trip and needing to enter an address into your GPS to arrive at your desired destination. The GPS will provide you with the step by step directions needed to get there. You then must prepare, not only for the trip, but for what you need when you arrive at your destination. Liken this to the **three P's** required to achieve your goal. The destination is your **Purpose**, the direction is your **Plan**, and the **Preparation** is for your arrival once the opportunity to achieve your goal is presented to you.

The philosopher Seneca said, "Luck is what happens when preparation meets opportunity." Some call it luck, some call it success. Whatever you call it, the point is that you not only have to prepare yourself in advance, such that you can be ready when opportunity presents itself, but most importantly, you must act and walk through the door when opportunity knocks. Bad luck, in my opinion, is the decision to **not** act on opportunities when they are presented to you, or the inability to take advantage of them because you were not prepared.

Success doesn't happen overnight. If you act and follow the instructions, you'll get there. The power is in the plan! Become successful in accomplishing your personal and professional goals by thinking, understanding, preparing, and acting (all wisely).

THE FIRST P - *PURPOSE*

So, we have all heard of the law of attraction: utilizing the power of your mind to get what you want. It responds to your thoughts which have frequencies that come back to you; like attracts like. This means that we should focus on good things versus bad things, positive versus negative, and more importantly what we want versus what we don't want. That last piece is absolutely critical because the law of attraction gives us whatever we think about or whatever we focus on. As a result, if we are constantly thinking about what we don't want, that's exactly what's going to come to us—the very thing that we don't want. Your future is created by your daily thoughts. This is where your vision and purpose come into play. The first decision I needed to make in order to achieve my goal was to clearly define my purpose.

At that time, I was in a project management role as an individual contributor at a large Fortune 10 company. I knew I wanted to join the coveted ranks of director, but I didn't put much thought into what type of director. Frankly, I really didn't care. Since my skillset was so diverse, I knew I could become a director of project management, director of sales, director of business development, director of sales operations... take your pick. I was qualified for multiple roles, but there were three problems with my approach.

First, I hadn't specified exactly what I wanted to do, which not only prevented the universe from engaging but also prevented me from creating a plan. I hadn't narrowed down a specific destination; therefore, I couldn't input it into the GPS. Instead of me saying I needed directions to Sacramento, I said I wanted to travel to the west coast. Second, my desires and thoughts were focused on where I did *not* want to be instead of where I wanted to be. There is a difference. A lot of us want to go somewhere else only because we don't like where we are. We can describe all the details of why we hate our current state of being but have a difficult time articulating our desired state. As a result, what's dominating our thoughts are the things that we don't want, versus what we want, which prevents us from breaking out of our current situation. Third, I needed to engage in self-reflection to determine what I was passionate about. I had to ask myself what motivated me and brought joy and fulfillment to my life.

When that clicked for me, I immediately took inventory of my innate and dominant gifts. Throughout my career, I had been on very few teams where the leader created a positive, innovative, empowering culture. I decided that I wanted to lead a strategic team engaging sales expertise, project management, operational excellence, and value proposition design to bridge the gap between client needs and delivery of key initiatives while maximizing the customer experience. More importantly, I wanted to drive employee engagement and allow people to bring their best selves to work, which would yield happy, productive employees that are vested in helping the company achieve its objectives. I discovered my purpose!

Next, not only did I write out my purpose, but I painted the picture in my mind and visualized what being in a role like that would look like. Doing that gave me confidence to conquer the fear of the unknown and fueled my desire and determination with a greater will to succeed. Why? Because I could taste and feel what previously was so vague and seemed out of reach. My purpose dominated my thoughts. I acted by putting those thoughts and feelings into the universe so they could be attracted to me. I then focused on what I could do right now. I didn't worry about what happened in the past or what could happen in the future because I could only control what I did at that exact moment! My actions created leverage to build momentum and propel me into my future. They gave me everything I needed to move on to the next P of success, Plan, and build the roadmap to my destination!

THE SECOND P - PLAN

A plan is just that, a roadmap. It is detailed, step by step instructions. It requires discipline and accountability to execute. We've all heard the adage, "If you fail to plan, you plan to fail." A well laid out plan is not optional, it is essential. This is usually the most difficult component of the system because we have a hard time figuring out exactly what to do or where to start. Start by studying the habits of successful individuals who have accomplished what you want to achieve. To help lay out your plan, consider visiting **www.sandysandersconsulting.com** to download a free Quick Start Guide. One valuable resource I found was Harvey Coleman's book, *Empowering Yourself: The Organizational Game Revealed* which describes P.I.E. (Performance, Image, and Exposure) as the three important keys to advancement. Harvey indicated that we need top notch performance to get in the game. Performance unlocks the door, although it only represents 10 percent of the pie. What's more important than just being a top performer is creating an outstanding image, 30 percent, with exposure being the most important element, representing 60 percent. You may have heard the phrase, "It's not what you know, it's who you know." Harvey goes a step further to point out that it's not who you know, but it's who knows you and what they know about you. My long-term plan had to account for all of those elements.

As a certified project management professional (PMP), I knew I had to break my plan down into smaller, bite-sized SMART goals in six-week intervals. SMART goals are specific, measurable, achievable, relevant, and time-bound. This is very important because patience is necessary to actively wait for your dream to come to pass, requiring maturity along with the understanding that there will be no instant gratification. My plan included tasks that were assigned time blocks on my calendar to prioritize completion. For example, below is a simple plan for one of my earlier six-week goals.

SIX-WEEK GOAL:

Find a mentor by April 15

- **Daily** – Meditate for 15 minutes on my purpose
- **Week 1** – Begin drafting a one-page personal value proposition (PVP) describing my aspirations
- **Week 2** – Develop my PVP by adding my background, personal brand, and leadership competencies
- **Week 3** – Seek feedback from leadership and peers on my PVP and make appropriate revisions
- **Week 4** – Research and schedule to participate in networking events or professional

development sessions that will have leaders who are potential mentors in attendance

- **Week 5** – Secure contact information of leaders or potential mentors
- **Week 6** – Email leaders or potential mentors to follow up or introduce myself and request 15-20 minutes for a mentoring moment, attaching my PVP

The six-week interval enables you to measure success and express gratitude for small accomplishments. It also motivates you to continue your journey. If you encounter roadblocks, just adjust the plan as this is a living, breathing, iterative process.

THE THIRD P - *PREPARATION*

Preparation helps you continue to build upon your plan. As you achieve certain milestones, your plan continues to evolve based on your learnings. Harvey Coleman said, "In order to advance, you must be fluent in the next level's language. Fluency is the ability to communicate and fit into an environment without conscious thought." This means you must be prepared to operate at the level that you are trying to achieve. As mentioned earlier, one of the first things I did to prepare myself for my next level was to seek counsel. I sought out people—mentors, coaches, and ultimately sponsors—who have accomplished more than I hoped to accomplish. I followed their guidance on ways to showcase my performance, build my brand, and make sure that the right people who could influence my career knew who I was.

I took several actions to prepare for the next level. One of which was having very specific and regularly scheduled conversations with my leadership to ensure that I knew exactly what expectations and objectives I needed to achieve in order to receive the highest possible performance rating. I also used my PVP as my talk track to highlight my brand when sitting down with executives and mentors. In addition, I created visibility for myself by volunteering for projects, holding leadership positions in Employee Resource Groups, and serving on boards of community organizations. One of my leaders said you should always sharpen your saw and remove any reason for someone to say you aren't ready for the next level; therefore, I added self-investment to the plan and obtained my MBA, PMP Certification, and Six Sigma Green Belt.

I think one of the most valuable lessons I learned during my preparation was to become a great problem solver. The problems you solve will determine the amount of money you make. The bigger the problems you solve, the more money you will make. You will also create a reputation that will place you in high demand. **The 3 P's to Success—Purpose, Plan, and Preparation**—was the key to me being sought after for my previous five roles in corporate America, the last three of which were director roles, due to my reputation! From 2013 to 2017, I advanced from an individual contributor to multiple roles of increasing leadership responsibility, finally leading a team of over 400 employees, driving engagement, growing the business, delivering top notch results, and ultimately achieving my purpose!

Living the Call Through the Power of Faith

Rev. Sharron Medley

"… Just as he chose us in Christ before the foundation of the world to be holy and blameless before him in love."
–Ephesians 1:4

I first felt "the call" to ministry in St. Joachim Catholic Church on the Southside of Chicago in about 1986. My children were attending the elementary school and we were required to attend church services on Family Sunday. I remember sitting in the pew on several Family Sundays and thinking that this was a place where I felt the presence of God and it moved me a great deal. That stirring, that feeling, made me want to do more with my life, but I did not know what to do or how to go about doing it. The feeling became stronger after witnessing the installation of a new priest. I watched that man prostrate himself before God. Offering himself on the altar openly, honestly, sincerely, and without reservation. How could I do the same? Again, I felt that there was something more I could and should do with my life. It felt like there was a deep hole on the inside of me and it made me continuously weepy. I felt pulled from the inside out; it was strange and almost painful. I needed someone to explain to me what was happening, but I didn't know how to put into words what I was experiencing. I went to see one of the priests and asked what I needed to do to become a member of the church. It was not to be. When I revealed that I had been divorced, he told me that I could not be considered as a candidate for membership. I felt hurt, sad, and totally let down. I didn't understand how I could just be turned away. How could someone who was a man of God turn away a person with a need to know God? Wasn't that their job? Weren't they supposed to work for God and nurture the flock? Weren't they supposed to bring souls to God and rescue them from sin? I didn't know what to do. I didn't know who to turn to. No one understood what I was going through and that didn't help. I didn't quite understand how a church could do something like that. I was hurt and confused and stopped attending church. I was invited by friends to their churches, but for years I said no; and when I did go, I did not have the same experience. I did not feel God in their places of worship. I didn't associate my hurt feelings with my lack of feeling. I began to fear that God did not love me. How could God love me when I had, according to the priest, broken God's commandments and I was not good enough to become one of His children? No one explained to me that I was already a child of God and even if they had I probably wouldn't have believed them, not really. I tried my best to bury the incident and move on, but the feelings did not go away. Suppressing those inner urgings to tell the world what had occurred with the Catholic Church was not an easy task but I thought, at that time, that was what I had to do in order to move forward with my life. I did not realize that I was hurting more than I knew. I did not attend church for almost five or six years. I was, however, drawn back following an extremely traumatic experience.

My marriage had imploded, which was devastating. I had made some bad life decisions and didn't know how to recover. I was in a new job as a network administrator which was way over my head. Because of my personal problems, I was having trouble focusing on my work.

One day while home alone, I felt (rather than heard) the instructions form within me that told me I needed to go to church. I remember asking out loud, "What is church going to do for me now when I have been let down in the past?" I ignored the prompting for several weeks until I was invited to church by a dear friend who knew of the events taking place in my life. One day while we were having lunch together, she turned to me and said, "Girl, you need to go to church." I didn't like the idea and thought I had given her my best argument; church was not the place for me. I told her that I had thought about it a little, but I had decided against it. "And," I asked, "what church would I go to?" She mentioned the name of a prominent church on the Southside of Chicago. Some of my family members attended that church, but I was not sure that I wanted to go there. I thought about it for a couple of weeks and realized that I needed to be fed. I had a decision to make and I felt a sense of urgency which meant I needed to make one fast. I decided to go. At first, I did not let my family know that I was there. I went with my friend and we sat in the balcony.

Initially, I was afraid. I didn't think I would get struck by lightning or anything, but I was concerned about how I would feel. How would I react to God and how would God react to me? I didn't have to wait long in order to find out. That first Sunday, my life was coming from the podium. It was as if the minister had lived with me the previous week. Over the course of several weeks, no matter who was speaking, the messages seemed to have been written especially for me. They spoke to me, affected me deeply, and provided the answers I needed at the time. It happened so much that my friend turned to me one Sunday and asked, "Do they know you here? This is really amazing that what you are going through is being talked about almost every Sunday." I started to feel the stirrings again, but life was much too traumatic to deal with them for too long. That continued for well over a year.

I knew I was in the right place because each Sunday I felt as if I was having a one-on-one conversation with the minister. During that year, the conversations continued without missing a beat. I took a couple of classes at the church and learned that before my life and circumstances could change, I had to make some changes first. I had to challenge my beliefs about myself, God, and the world. I worked with a minister to try to understand what I needed to do and how I could go about it. The minister just told me in a very glib way to pray about it. "Ok," I asked, "what does that mean? How do I do that?" The minister suggested that I repeat The Lord's Prayer over and over silently until I felt a sense of peace. Well, I tried that for a while, but it did not work well for me. I finally had a long talk with my mother, and she told me to purchase the book *All the Promises of the Bible* by Herbert Lockyer. She also recommended the book *The Dynamic Laws of Healing* by Catherine Ponder. In the book, Ms. Ponder suggests that forgiveness is one of the keys to healing. Forgiveness? Who did I need to forgive? Well, the Catholic Church for one and myself for another. I had allowed someone else to define who I was and how I was to live, and that was not a good thing. I lived in fear of a God that I thought didn't love me nor want me, and I had allowed fear to rule my life. I lived in fear of discovery, and I acted like everything was ok, but it was not. The fear of change had a grip on me. Fear was all around me. Fear, fear, fear. So, something had to change. I read through both books and began to formulate a plan. I needed to forgive myself but not dwell on the past. I needed to determine what I really believed. Did I believe that God had turned me away or that man had turned me away? Did I believe the promises of God that I had read or was I content to live in fear and think that I was being punished? I needed to start from the ground level and determine what I believed.

To start, I developed a prayer, forgiveness, and gratitude program for myself. I used the book containing the promises of God. God is the Father and I am the son. We are all sons. God is the Source of all, and I am made from that Source. That being the case and the truth, what exactly was my problem? I wanted to get better and decided to put the plan into action. My prayer, forgiveness, and gratitude program started with 15 minutes of prayer time and 15 minutes of quiet meditation. The prayer time was used to focus on the promises, as I did not have the capacity at the time to pray on my own. Next, I took one of the forgiveness statements from *The Dynamic Laws of Healing* and repeated it slowly several times each morning. At the recommendation of a friend, I also began a gratitude journal and listed five things I was grateful for each day. I took two of the promises of God from the book and wrote them on index cards. I carried one card in my planner, one in my car, and I put one in my desk drawer at work. The promises that I selected were as follows:

One: "He that dwelleth in the secret place of the most High shall abide under the shadow of the Almighty."—Psalm 91:1. I needed to pray. I needed to commune with God. But I was not confident that prayer was the solution and I was not really feeling it.

Two: "If ye bide in me, and my words abide in you, ye shall ask what ye will, and it shall be done unto you."—John 15:7. You see, the book by Catherine Ponder, *The Dynamic Laws of Healing*, provided some information and instructions on how to change my thinking. She indicated that if a person could change the way they think and feel, they could change their lives entirely. One of the steps required was to have faith. Hebrews 11:1 says, "Faith is the substance of things hoped for..." Hope is a form of expectation. As I looked at my life, it was apparent that my expectations were not very good and were causing a great disturbance. I learned that my dominant patterns of thought would eventually show up in my life, and they most certainly had. I thought that it was my fault that my marriage was ending. I believed that there was something broken inside of me that prevented me from finding real love, real success, and real happiness.

Since my thinking controlled my life and my belief system controlled my thinking, the question was how could the words of the Lord abide in me? How could I change my thinking so that I could find a sense of peace and move forward? How could I see the TRUTH and not see just through my physical eyes? How could I release the fear that had been controlling my life for so many years? The answer was focus. My focus had been on the wrong things. Scripture states in Isaiah 26:3, "Thou wilt keep him in perfect peace, whose mind is stayed on thee: because he trusteth in thee." That was the question wasn't it? Did I trust God?

I'm happy to report that my prayer, forgiveness, and gratitude program worked. Over time, I was able to change my focus through prayer, which is "communion with God that takes place at the innermost part of man's being." (*The Revealing Word*, Charles Fillmore). I spent a great deal of time just talking to and with God. Yes, there were times that I didn't think I was getting through to myself, but I persisted. I changed my focus through forgiveness; giving up the past, resentment, and fear; and, I ceased feeling resentful toward God and the Catholic Church. During that period of introspection, I came to understand that there is more than one road and I was just on another path. I changed my focus through gratitude—being grateful for the life I was living and the people in it. My marriage ended (sometimes relationships end), but I triumphed through remaining faithful to the process and steadfast when tempted to give up.

I know that God is and because God is, I am. Faith, prayer, forgiveness, and gratitude are the action steps to take when your life seems to have no meaning and fear is guiding you. Ask yourself, "What do I believe?" If the answer to the questions is, "I don't know," then be faithful, pray, forgive, and be grateful.

Attention Please: This Is NOT a Dress Rehearsal!

Toni Holden-McGee

Attention please: this is NOT a dress rehearsal! This was the thought that was going through my mind as my truck flipped in a double rollover crash in the spring of 2018. Although upon impact, I didn't feel like my life was over, I wanted the car to stop rolling! I will come back to that tragic moment later in this chapter. There are three P's that prompted me to write my story: Passion, Position, and Purpose.

I have not always had a passion for living life. Although my childhood had more happy and joyful days than challenging days, those challenging days had me thinking otherwise. My parents love my brother and I more than life itself, but during their dissolution of marriage, he and I moved around a lot in a two to three-year time span. Though brief, during those times of moving from place to place, I felt more like a chess piece than a human being. My mother, brother, and I continued to go to church on Sundays, where I received some guidance and hope. My mother introduced me to the Lord at the early age of eight and I gave my life to Him at age eleven. By the time I reached my teenage years, I honestly didn't believe God was anywhere in my corner! I knew He still existed, but I felt like He wasn't rooting for me. Or was it that I wasn't rooting for Him? As my outlook on life seemed to improve after a few years of moving around amongst family and neighbors, I found a new joy and appreciation for my life. I've always been close to both of my parents but during their separation period, my brother and I lived with my mother. Then, from our teenage years into early adulthood, we lived with my father. With the move to my father's home, stability was re-established and school friendships formed. A sense of feeling like a typical teenager developed, which was comforting. Not to mention that I had the opportunity to build a stronger relationship with my father and spend time doing interesting activities with him. Those activities included frequenting estate sales and checking out doll shows. I began to view my life from the perspective of what I could do to improve my shortcomings and support others who might be going through doom and gloom.

I reconnected with the Lord and asked Him to fill me with inspiration, give me a zest for living, and allow me to be an inspiration to others. My requests were fulfilled almost immediately. As my outlook on life improved, my overall health, wellness, and a sense of purpose developed. I've always had the will to feel good about myself, something my mother instills in me even to this day. I enjoy making other people smile and feel good about themselves as it is a reflection of how I feel about myself. I relish in the good times (making great memories to look back on), and I always remember that God has me no matter what happens! Talking to people about their life's journey, how they got where they are, and listening to their stories is what keeps my passion on fire! My goodness, everyone has problems! But how you deal with those problems is a direct link to how you will deal with successes and failures down the road and how you will help others see the light during difficult situations. My passion stays lit because I remain connected to God who allows me to connect to other people; we share our life stories! Every day I am blessed to start over and make a difference in someone's life. That feeling is immeasurable!

This brings me to the second P; Position. My position in life is not one of appointment through job opportunity but a spiritual assignment. I am at a place in my life where I know I can make change happen by using my voice. My position in life is quite different from my purpose in life. I believe that God has positioned me to be a tough woman, not only in my daily professional life but in my family. I am the strong one in the family. I am the one who will seek out opportunities to make finances and academia work, tweak my health and wellness needs to make me work, and push the family to pursue outside interests that we would otherwise not do, to make us work! I get a kick out of stepping out of my box and breaking the boredom of the everyday routine of going to work, working out, cooking, going over homework, etc.

I easily get bored with the humdrum of an everyday routine. I am the adventurous one in the household, and I will drag everyone with me who is willing to take a chance to go out and have some outdoor fun and excitement! As a child, I enjoyed catching snakes, butterflies, grasshoppers, and anything else buggy! I still enjoy that hobby although I don't get much time to relish in it now that I am a responsible adult and parent. I wasn't then and I'm still not afraid of getting dirty. I enjoy putting my hands in the dirt, fixing machines to make them run again, and taking apart machines to see how each part is dependent on the other for functionality.

My curiosity has always gotten the best of me. As a child, I would wander off from the family, get lost in the grocery store, and then cry to death for one of my parents to find me. You think I would have learned my lesson. Now that I'm an adult, I have often thought of the various positions in life that I've held. I am brave, confident, curious, and resilient. I will persevere until I get the job done. I am on an emotional roller coaster at times trying to balance work, parenting, schooling, and marriage but after some self-care (body massages and exercise fitness routines), I can manage life. These traits describe my personality; they have formed and shaped me into the strong woman I am today. God has me positioned in the right place at the right time, every time. Even though I may feel a bit out of sorts or I cannot quite grasp why I always seem like the chosen one to go through drama, at this point in my life, I asked myself, "Why not me?" God has been preparing me to play a significant role. He has carried me throughout my childhood challenges and has continued to bless my family and I with an abundance of health, wealth, great job opportunities, and the chance to meet amazing people. No one but the

Lord has allowed me to write this chapter in hopes of inspiring others to push forward in life and leave self-doubt behind!

Reflecting on my childhood and looking at my life now, I continue to challenge myself physically. I have completed the Tough Mudder Mud Race involving a 10-mile run and 20 obstacle courses along the way. The race was challenging but fun and rewarding at the same time! There were only three of us on the team, but we depended on one another throughout the race and completed it together. I also participated in two bikini challenges within the last couple of years. Not only did I make my goal, but I surpassed it with pounds and inches lost and I gained muscle, confidence, inspiration, and a greater appreciation for the human mind, body, and soul! The women I worked out with came with their stories; we shared, prayed, and then we got busy and made the dream work. Once you get your mind right, everything else falls into place.

If I were helping a friend on a journey like the one I described in this chapter, I would encourage that person to see the possibilities in their circumstance by telling him or her that the Lord has positioned them so they can be of influence for the greater good, make change happen, and be a blessing to others by making their lives greater and inspiring them to know that YES, THEY CAN accomplish their dreams and hit their target. And, YES THEY WILL continue to press forward and move beyond fear of the unknown . I would also say to that person that God has their best interest in mind and only He can and will create their life's journey. He can make it better than they could have ever imagined or created for themselves!

This brings me back to the beginning of this chapter when I spoke about that awful car accident and the third P; Purpose. One of the scariest situations I ever faced was that double rollover crash in the spring of 2018. Although I felt no fear during the actual flipping of the truck, fear crept in as I kept telling myself, *You know you just crawled out of that vehicle unharmed.* Your mind will play dirty tricks on you if you don't have enough Jesus juice to clean up those ugly thoughts! At that moment, when the truck stopped rolling and was in an upside-down position, I realized that I needed a life readjustment.

I felt no pain, and I did not doubt that I was going to get out of that truck alive. I felt well protected, and I'm not just talking about the seatbelt that held my body snug either! There was a phenomenal presence in and around the truck that I could feel. When the vehicle stopped moving, I looked for a way to get out. There was one window. It was the front passenger window and it had shattered upon impact. I unhooked my seatbelt, shook my body to check for pain, and then immediately turned my body so that I could crawl backward out of the window. I crawled out as quickly as I could, stood up next to the vehicle, and retrieved my fitness workout bag as I had just had a heart-pumping work out that morning and was heading back to the house to start my workday.

Fearlessness is often described as an emotion experienced in anticipation of some specific pain or danger. Fearlessness is also described as one without fear, heroism, bravery, courageousness, heart, and soul. I indeed felt all of the traits of fearlessness after I walked away from my totaled truck with my life! As I reminisce on that day, I couldn't help but ask myself and my family, "Why me? How did I survive such a horrific automobile accident without being injured?" According to rollover fatality statistics by the National Highway Traffic Safety Administration (NHTSA), in 2010 alone, more than 7,600 people died in rollover crashes and rollovers accounted for nearly 35 percent of all deaths from passenger vehicle crashes. The majority of the passengers who died, 69 percent, were not wearing seatbelts (Yoon, Lee & Ahn, 2013). I want to add that although I was wearing a seatbelt, God definitely had a hand in rescuing me from being another statistic. I wonder if those people, who like me walked away from double rollover crash accidents, attribute their safety to God saving them or them saving themselves? I was back to driving, working out, and working as usual within 24-48 hours as though nothing had happened to me at all.

I am a living witness to others, and I know it. If nothing about my story resonates with you, I want you to know that YOU ARE NOT IN CONTROL! There is a higher authority in charge. The sooner you realize that, the sooner you will see your life differently. It's not about you, your social media presence, your occupational position, your annual salary, or all of the other materialistic things we indulge in every day.

There is a reason why you and I are still on the face of this earth, and it is to live life through a selfless lens. We are here to offer ourselves as living witnesses and to rely on God's Word that He will take care of us and our needs. I still struggle with letting go and letting God, but I am trying every day. I am pushing beyond fear, remaining consistent in listening to God about why He has put me on this earth, and gaining the understanding that I am a vessel. I am still learning about what I am supposed to yield, how I can be of service to others, and how I can fulfill my interests and dreams.

Attention please: this is not a dress rehearsal. There are no tryouts or do-overs. We only have this one shot at life to get it wrong, to get it right, and to understand what purpose God has for us. I'm not striving for perfection, but I am aiming for peace of mind and purpose driven opportunities that will guide my life's position and continue to fuel my passion. I do believe that God has a plan for all of us. I'm still learning and working on my life's plan. I am a purpose driven woman. Stay in tune and remain humble!

About the Authors

Felicia Shakespeare is a leadership coach, an author, an entrepreneur, an international speaker, and an accomplished educator who is on a mission to inspire others to be intentional about living a life of faith and purpose.

She is the 2019 recipient of the FWD Collective Award, 2019 nominee of the prestigious Global Woman Award, 2018 winner of the WNBA Chicago Sky #RedefinePossible Women's Leadership Award, and a 2017 Indie Author Legacy Awards Author of the Year Finalist for her book, *You Are Your Brand*. Felicia is also the creator of the women's mentorship community mClass: Master, Mentor, Motivate.

Felicia holds a bachelor of science in business, master of education in educational leadership, master of teaching, and a personal development coach certification. She is also the founder of The Purpose School and host of *A Purpose Driven Woman Podcast with Felicia Shakespeare*.

Felicia enjoys traveling, fine dining, and attending plays, movies, and concerts. She currently resides in Chicago, Illinois.

Learn more at www.apurposedrivenwoman.us

Bella Caetano, the founder and designer of Bellina Caetano, moved to Chicago from Brazil in 2016 to spark a movement aiming to change how the international community perceives Brazilian design, art, and culture. Bella designs, produces, and imports all of her products from Brazil with a noble mission of creating jobs back in her country. One of her most recent accomplishments was opening the first Brazilian boutique in Chicago, right on Michigan Avenue.

Bella serves as a board member of the Chicago-São Paulo Chapter of Partners of the Americas and is a volunteer and sponsor of the MOSTRA Brazilian Film Festival. Her motivated, social, and creative personality has led her to achieve many of her dreams. Despite having no formal education in jewelry, Bella has an education and background in architecture. Having learned a lot about design from her architecture classes, jewelry became the creative outlet that led to her path as a business owner and an active Brazilian ambassador.

Learn more at www.bellinacaetano.com

Charisma Smith is a results-driven leader who has spent the last twenty years breaking barriers in the real estate and construction industries. She seamlessly transitioned from corporate America to entrepreneurship. Today, she is the co-owner of a boutique real estate firm, a construction company, and an affordable housing non-profit organization. Her goal is to encourage entrepreneurs to follow their dreams by teaching them how to seize the moment.

Charisma values serving her community through church and as a member of the board of directors of the Canopy Realtor Association.

A graduate from the University of North Carolina at Charlotte, Charisma holds a certificate in construction management from North Carolina State University. She has also participated in various diversity leadership programs and is an executive life coach.

To connect, email her at charismadockery@gmail.com

Erika "Birdie" Shavers is known as Birdie because she loves the game of golf. A native Chicagoan, Erika is currently the volunteer coordinator and assistant program director for an international junior golf organization. Her story is remarkable because of how her passion for the game of golf became the lifeline she used to pull herself through financial hardship perpetuated by the real estate recession that began in 2007. Erika is a member of Alpha Kappa Alpha Sorority, Inc.

Erika serves as an honorary member of the South Shore Ladies Golf League and was previously a member of the Women's Golf Club Columbus Park (WGCCP). She is also the founder of Ladies on the Green Golf League. Her most recent accomplishment is the creation of Swing Easy Golf™.

Erika has taught close to 100 clients in her spare time and for the past seven seasons has enjoyed being a CPS high school golf coach. The next step in her progression is to become an LPGA certified golf instructor.

To connect, email her at
swingeasygolflessons@gmail.com

Joyce Dawkins, aka Simply Joy, is the founder and CEO of She ROCKS It. She ROCKS It is an organization that was purposely designed to host events that honor and empower women all over the world. SRIs featured events include: The Celebrating Women Who ROCK Gala, The Girlfriend Gathering, and The SHE Lounge Experience.

Simply Joy has a B.A. in political science and sociology, a M.A. in organizational leadership/higher education, and a degree in coaching. She is the creator of the online blog: *My Soul Point of View* and the online group: I AM SHE. She is also a member of Delta Sigma Theta Sorority, Inc.

Simply Joy has been featured on *The JAM Morning Show* and in *COFFEA Magazine, VoyageChicago Magazine, Sistah's Place Magazine*, and *Love Black Chicago Magazine*. She is the recipient of both a Phenomenal Black Woman Award and a G.E.M.S. Award.

Learn more at www.sherocksit.com

Kathleen Quinn is the founder and owner of CFOQuinn, a consulting firm focused on helping small to medium sized businesses maximize financial results and accelerate growth. Since 2013, she has worked with a number of startups in the Chicago area. Previously, she worked for several Fortune 500 companies as well as a European-based specialty food company and began her career in public accounting.

She is a graduate of the University of Illinois at Urbana-Champaign MBA program and Albion College from which she holds a bachelor of arts in economics. She is also a registered certified public accountant.

Kathleen, her husband, two children, and their goofy dog live outside of Chicago and enjoy spending time on the Les Cheneaux Islands where they can be found sailing, swimming, and reading.

Learn more at www.cfoquinn.com

LaTonya Forrest was born and raised in Chicago, Illinois. She is a single mother of four children, and her greatest joy and accomplishment is raising them.

LaTonya obtained her associate degree in general business from Malcolm X College and her bachelor of science degree in technical management with an emphasis in small business management and entrepreneurship from DeVry University.

She is a member of Sigma Beta Delta, an international honor society for business management and administration. She is also a member of an outstanding church in Chicago where she serves on various ministries including the choir, praise team, and the outreach ministry. LaTonya has also served as lead servant of the nursing home ministry as well as choir director and teacher in the children's church ministry.

LaTonya works in public service as a rehabilitation case coordinator, assisting individuals with disabilities in obtaining home services. She is passionate about helping and serving others.

To connect, email her at LForrest24@yahoo.com

Lesley Martinez, MS MRKT, PhD candidate, is the founder and president of ADVZOR, a digital marketplace and
contractor agency for service-based professionals to grow
their consultation business and thrive in this twenty-first
century economy. As a community psychologist and equi-
ty designer, Lesley is committed to globally marginalized
community development and economic sustainability
through tech-enabled entrepreneurship and digital and
media literacy. Her core research topics include access to
capital for black women and economic autonomy.

Learn more at www.advzor.com/lesleyme

Liane Williams is a wife, mother, and entrepreneur. A graduate of Illinois Wesleyan University, she has worked for State Farm Insurance for nearly 35 years, the last 24 as an agent. She enjoys using her voice in any way she can, whether to encourage others or in song. Liane has been singing and performing since she was a child and loves singing all types of music, especially gospel and jazz. Acting has always been a passion of hers, both on stage in musical theater and as a voice over actor. Over the past ten years, Liane has also branched off into real estate investing and is proud to provide others with quality housing, helping them go from tenants to homeowners.

Liane's family is what she is most proud of and being a wife for 23 years and the mother of two sons has been her most fulfilling accomplishment.

To connect, email her at lianewilliams@msn.com

Molly Hebda is the owner and chief dreamer of the boutique photography studio Motion Inspired and the founder of Women Making an Impact, a group that brings together local women in business to collaborate, support, and inspire.

Motion Inspired Studio, located in the historic downtown village of Lemont, Illinois, is where Molly wields her superpower in encouraging women to step out as the face of their brand. Creating images through personal, intimate connection in a safe, open environment while building on her love of boudoir photography, she helps women business owners see themselves as powerful yet feminine individuals in their field. Molly's work was recently featured in *Rizing Magazine*.

Molly's happy place is simply hanging out at home with her husband, son, and rescue pup, Pepperoni (aptly named after she was found at Pizza Hut!), with a good Gin in hand and something delicious cooking on the grill.

Learn more at www.motioninspired.com

Muhjah Stewart McCaskill is a social entrepreneur, mentor, motivational speaker, and community advocate whose non-profit organization, Strengthening A Nation (focused on entrepreneurship training and workshops for at-risk populations in Chicago) has reached over 150 youth. Muhjah believes in the population she serves and is dedicated to shifting the entrepreneurial gap in the communities of Chicago and reducing the school to prison pipeline by teaching financial literacy and entrepreneurship.

Muhjah holds a bachelor of science in business management. She has been honored to receive the following: Award for Community Leadership (Wearing Big Hats, 2019) and Woman of Excellence Award (*Chicago Defender*, 2018). She currently serves on the board for the AFCA Baseball League (Athletes for Christ Association) and was inducted into the Delta Mu Delta International Honor Society for Business at Chicago State University in 2009.

Learn more at www.strengtheninganation.org

Sandy Sanders is an entrepreneur and business leader who is passionate about empowering others, through leadership and career coaching, to tap into their innate talents and potential and transform their personal and professional lives. She is an expert at building high performing teams and helping sales organizations achieve operational excellence.

As an influential trailblazer of change for several Fortune 100 companies including IBM, American Express, MetLife, and AT&T, Sandy was honored with an Outstanding Career Achievement STEM Award by *Women of Color Magazine*. She holds a bachelor's in marketing from The Ohio State University, an MBA from Florida State University, a project management professional certification (PMP), a Six Sigma Green Belt, and a cybersecurity certification.

Sandy has a zeal for giving back through mentorship and serving on community and employee resource group boards, earning her five President's Volunteer Service Awards. She is a proud mother of two, enjoys international travel, and resides in Florida.

Learn more at www.sandysandersconsulting.com

Rev. Sharron Medley is a licensed and ordained minister and teacher. She has taught classes for the Johnnie Theological Seminary and various churches, and offers online classes through Spiritual Lifesavers, Inc. She attended Chicago State University and is currently working toward a bachelor's degree in metaphysics through the University of Metaphysics. Her professional background is in information technology and insurance.

Reverend Sharron is currently the founder and director of Spiritual Lifesavers, an online ministry designed to help individuals uplift, empower, and transform themselves through the practical application of spiritual principles. The lifesavers used are The Fruit of the Spirit, The Beatitudes, and The Ten Commandments, metaphysically interpreted. Spiritual Lifesavers offers an inspirational blog, classes, workshops, and spiritual coaching all designed to uplift, empower, and transform!

Reverend Sharron is the mother of three daughters, a proud grandmother, and a great-grandmother.

Learn more at www.spirituallifesavers.com

Toni Holden-McGee is a digital learning coordinator, digital learning instructor, and FAB Lab technology designer who volunteers at the Museum of Science and Industry and serves on the District 97 iLearn Technology Advisory committee. Toni holds a bachelor's degree in computer information science and management and a master's degree in management information systems with a specialization in digital media. She is currently pursuing a doctorate degree in information technology.

Toni's career experience spans through years of working in the information science and education technology sectors for non-profit organizations and sharing her passion with young and old about STEAM programming and educations technology research. She is best known for providing digital learning programs and technical support strategies that will continue to inspire others to never stop learning!

Toni and her husband are raising their energetic son. Together they enjoy new travel experiences, outdoor adventures, and loving life.

To connect, email her at holden_toni@hotmail.com